Fact or Fantasy

FACT
OR
FANTASY

The Authenticity of the Gospels

DAVID C. C. WATSON

H. E. WALTER LTD

First published in 1980 by
H. E. Walter Ltd
26 Grafton Road, Worthing
West Sussex BN11 1QU, England

© D. C. C. Watson 1980

ISBN 0 85479 022 5

Printed in Great Britain by
Billing & Sons Ltd, Guildford and London

To the Headquarters Staff of the
Leprosy Mission, London
whose kindness and encouragement made
possible the writing of this book.

Contents

MAP

Acknowledgements

Quotations from three modern writers are liberally sprinkled at chapter headings. They are C. S. Lewis's urbane but devastating attack on Bultmann's myth-mythology, *Fern-seed and Elephants* (Collins); Dorothy L. Sayers' *The Man Born to be King* (Gollancz) which ran through 24 impressions in 26 years and V. Messori's excellent up-to-date defence of the Gospels, *Jesus Hypotheses* (St. Paul Publications).

This threefold cord is not quickly broken. The Professor, the detective-novel writer and the journalist all agree that our Gospels cannot possibly be the product of enthusiasm, invention or accretion. All agree that the words are the words of Jesus, and the miracles are historical fact.

Preface

The task of an apologist is not enviable. He may be stigmatized as 'merely negative'. An Indian proverb says, 'It is better to light a lamp than curse the darkness'; and with this sentiment we heartily concur. Nevertheless, as Paul reminds us, in a great house many kinds of vessel are needed — dust pans as well as bone china. It is my hope that these chapters may help to clear away some of the rubbish that has accumulated in Britain over the past 70 years. I leave to others the higher tasks of evangelism and the writing of better commentaries.

Contrary to what some may think, I bear no malice towards those whose books I feel compelled to criticise. I fully realise that they represent a *school* of thought, and many other commentators say much the same. It just happens that these four are the ones I have come across as an RE teacher.

On the other hand it is noticeable that in the Bible it is often not individuals but *groups* that are condemned e.g. for taking away the key of knowledge and hindering those who wish to enter the Kingdom. As there is a fellowship of light, so there is a conspiracy of darkness. And when I reflect that in hundreds of schools all over Britain, thousands of innocent children are being taught things which simply are not true, I cannot but feel that 'modern scholars' as a group resemble all too closely the false prophets of Jeremiah's day and the false teachers foretold by St. Peter (2:3). This 'Year of the Child', 1979, affords a good opportunity to consider our ways and ponder again the solemn warning of Christ:

'Whoever causes one of these little ones who believe in me to stumble, it would be better for him to have a great millstone fastened round his neck and to be drowned in the depth of the sea.' (Matthew 18:6).

Easter, 1979   D.C.C.W.

Introduction

The purpose of this book is to establish what has been believed by 99.9% of all Christendom for 95% of the Christian era — that our four Gospels were written respectively by Matthew and John, apostles, by Mark the companion of Peter and by Luke the companion of Paul.

The error which I seek to correct, though born in Germany, now flourishes mainly in the English-speaking world. Of those Christians who speak the other 1630 languages in which the Gospels circulate, very few have leisure to bother their heads about authorship. The sacred books are so obviously different from all other books, their message so satisfies the deepest spiritual needs, that they are usually accepted without question as the Word of God. Believers in China painstakingly record the precious words from slow radio broadcasts. The underground churches in Russia pass around their pathetically worn copies to be copied yet again by hand. But in the West, where we have 50 different English versions of the Bible, amid the luxuriance of scholarship grow many poisonous weeds. These have a subtly numbing effect on Christian work at home and abroad, as is shown by the following letter written in 1963 by a missionary in Pakistan:

'I'm afraid it will be some time before I *dare* to teach a course on the Gospels. What is the answer to the Synoptic Problem? . . .'

The writer was a Master of Arts and a Bachelor of Divinity. If these lines can save a few more B.D.'s or even non-professional Christians from such unnecessary headaches, I shall feel that my time has not been wasted.

Part Two is a summary of lectures given at the Bible Training Institute, Glasgow, 1961—64, and is intended for the serious Bible student. Part One reflects my experience as a

Lyons 1

Rome

Carthage 3

1 Pothinus, Irenæus.
2 Justin Martyr.
3 Tertullian.
4 Quadratus.
5 Tatian.
6 Polycarp, Irenæus.
7 John the Apostle.
8 Papias.

THE ROMAN EMPIRE

It has been estimated that 60,000 copies of the Gospels (mostly the Greek originals, but also Latin and Syriac versions) were circulating in the Roman Empire by 200 AD. (see p.29). This map shows how wide~spread was the witness to their authenticity.

Urfa 5 (Edessa)

Smyrna 6 Hierapolis 8

Ephesus 7

Athens 4

Antioch 9

Cæsarea 12
Samaria 10

Alexandria 11

9 Theophilus.

10 Justin Martyr.

11 Clement, Origen.

12 Eusebius.

teacher of R.E. 1971–76. Here, at least, the critics will be right in postulating an 'original' document, and a transposition of order.

CHAPTER ONE

Crossword, Gospels and other Puzzles

*'The expositor who nullifies the historical groundwork of
Scripture for the sake of finding only spiritual truths everywhere, brings death on all correct interpretations.'*
        John A. Bengel (1742 A.D.)

An apocryphal story is told about an old lady who did the
'Times' crossword in half an hour and 'got all the answers
wrong'. That was indeed a feat of genius. One would have
thought it impossible for one set of clues to yield two
totally different sets of answers, each set of words interlocking within itself. Yet they say it has been done.

More surprising still, however, is the fact that within the
last century one and the same set of 'clues' about our four
Gospels has yielded two totally different sets of answers, each
set apparently self-consistent but each set wholly excluding
the other. It is my purpose in this book to examine each set
and allow the reader to judge which answers are right and
which are wrong.

Go into any second-hand bookshop, ask for the theological
section, and pick out a commentary on the Gospels dated 1910
or earlier. Ten to one your commentator will allow that
Matthew the apostle wrote Matthew, Mark the companion of
Peter wrote Mark, Luke the companion of Paul wrote Luke,
and John the apostle wrote John. Such a book lies before me
now. Published at Cambridge by the University Press, entitled
The Gospel according to St. Matthew edited by the Rev. A.
Carr M.A., formerly Fellow of Oriel College, Oxford, and
dated 1908. Turning over we note that the first edition was
printed in 1878 and this is the *29th* edition in 30 years. Tens
of thousands of copies must have been sold and used in

scores of schools. A very large number of teachers must have examined it carefully and found it entirely satisfactory. And what does this Fellow of Oriel have to say about authorship?

'The authorship of the first Gospel has been ascribed by an unbroken tradition to the apostle Matthew.'

Now let us look at *The Gospel according to St. Matthew* published by the same CUP in 1963, reprinted 1972 and 1973, with a commentary by A. W. Argyle. On p.16 he states:

'The Gospel *cannot have been written by the apostle Matthew* because it is based upon the Gospel of Mark.'

In the course of our study we shall enquire into the validity of this judgment, but before leaving the Rev. A. Carr it is worth passing on his further comments which, we fear, those who share Mr. Argyle's view have too little considered:

'St. Matthew was an eye-witness of the events which he chronicles, yet it is often remarked that his descriptions are less graphic and full of detail than those of St. Mark, who wrote what he had heard from the lips of others. This need not be a matter of surprise. It is indeed a phenomenon that meets us every day. It is not the contemporary and the eye-witness but the historian of a succeeding age who takes the keenest interest in detail and records with faithful accuracy the less prominent circumstances of a great event. It is the Herodotus or the Macaulay . . . who gathers from every source materials for a minute and brilliant picture, rather than the actual spectator who is often too deeply absorbed by the one point of supreme interest to notice the looks and acts of other bystanders, or *so impressed by the speaker's glowing thoughts as to deem them alone worthy of record.*' (our italics)

But have not new literary finds and archaeological discoveries revolutionised Gospel criticism? Surely the clues today are *different*? If Mr. Carr were alive today, would he not agree with 'most modern scholars'? Well, I am no prophet but this much can be said: if Mr. Carr were to change his views it would *not* be because the clues have changed. In the last 100 years not one scrap of historical evidence has come to light which in any way tends to weaken the universal and unbroken tradition of Christendom — that Matthew wrote the first Gospel. The change is due not to new facts but to new fashions in thought; and what we have to decide is, does the new fashion fit the evidence better than the old?

Some wit once remarked that theologians spend their time answering questions which no one is asking. So our first enquiry will be:

Does it matter who wrote the Gospels?

With some kinds of book, authorship matters very little . . . log tables, for instance, or a French Grammar. What about Shakespeare? Some people still contend that Francis Bacon wrote the plays, and most of us would survive the shock if it were discovered tomorrow that he did. Why? Because plays are written to entertain, not to persuade or convert us. Or consider medicine: does it matter which doctor writes a prescription, provided the stuff works? Obviously not. Therefore, say some, it matters not who wrote Matthew, Mark, Luke and John. The message is there; believe it, obey it, and you will be saved, *whoever* the messenger was.

There is much truth in this. Probably 99.9% of all the people who have read Mark's Gospel worried not at all about the author. They accepted the book as Good News, became convinced by reading that Jesus is indeed the Son of God, and experienced pardon, peace, and power, through believing. However, there is still the one in a thousand who wants to get at the roots of things and have a sure intellectual basis for worship and service. If you are that one in a thousand, this book is written for you.

CHAPTER TWO

Why are the Gospels so short?

'There is light enough for those who want to believe, and darkness enough for those who do not.'

                                                                    Pascal

Mark's Gospel would just about fit onto the middle page of one of our full-size newspapers. Matthew is about half as long again (15,000 words) and Luke about 10% more than Matthew. This is an astonishing fact when we consider what they might have been. Most modern biographies run to about 150,000 words, i.e. ten times as long as Matthew. Charles de Gaulle's is 190,000, Randolph Churchill's about half that figure.

But are not modern parallels misleading? Did not Christ live in a non-literary age?

This is a common fallacy. Livy (died 17 A.D.) wrote a *History of Rome* in 142 books (no, not a misprint) — millions of words. The Jewish historian Josephus (90 A.D.) took ¾ million words to write his *Antiquities* and *Wars of the Jews;* and Plutarch's (100 A.D.) biography of Alexander the Great (who died at 33, like Jesus) is about 2½ times the length of Matthew.

At the risk of boring my readers, we shall embark on yet more mathematics for half a page. In my red-letter Bible I find 1530 verses spoken by the Lord Jesus Christ. Taking 16 as the average number of words to a verse, this gives a total of about 24,000 words — excluding Mark, which (as you know) has very few verses that do not correspond with Matthew or Luke. There are also many passages in Matthew and Luke which overlap, so 24,000 words is an absolute *maximum.*

Now compare this with Charles Spurgeon, the famous preacher. His recorded sermons (1861—1891) fill 62 volumes each of 700 pages and it is said that in tract form they would reach from here to the moon. But what about the orators of antiquity? Were they so prolific? Well, the published speeches and letters of Cicero (50 B.C.) run to well over a million words. So do the works of Plato (400 B.C.) and Aristotle (300 B.C.). So, if we were considering the possibilities of literary production in the first century A.D., there is no reason at all why our four Gospels could not have been twenty times as long as they are.

Now let us consider *how many words did Christ speak?* — in the course of His three year ministry.

John Wesley used to preach 15 sermons a week and covered 5000 miles a year on horseback. So it seems not unreasonable to suggest that Jesus may have preached for about 20 hours a week, = 1000 hours a year.

How many words an hour? Dr. Edward Norman in his Reith lectures averaged 130 w.p.m.; many Oriental preachers, and Dr. Billy Graham, are nearer 200. But let's put it at the slowest possible rate, say 50 w.p.m. Even this gives us 50 x 60 = 3000 words per hour

= 3 million words a year

= 9 million words in the three years.

If we halve this figure to guard against overstatement, we still have 4 million words to account for, and only 24,000 recorded.

Expressed as a fraction this will be $\frac{4000}{24} = \frac{500}{3} = .6\%$.

This means that out of every 500 words spoken by Christ, only three have been recorded! Never, perhaps, in the history of human speech, have so many words been condensed into so few.

This is the more remarkable when we reflect on who He claimed to be. If Jesus was indeed the eternal Son of God, creator of the world, then His words must be incomparably more important than all the poetry, all the plays, all the philosophy and all the history ever written by the hand of man. Surely we might have expected from Him a book at least as long as *Pilgrim's Progress?*

The answer, I believe, is threefold:

1. As Abraham Lincoln said, God must love the common

man, because He made so many of them. The vast majority
of mankind have little time or taste for serious reading, and if
each Gospel were as long as the Pelican Commentary on Mark
(458 pp) most of us would have given up Bible study long ago.
In fact God is merciful to our poor tired bodies, weak wills
and distracted minds, and the Gospels are so divided into short
self-contained passages that all four can easily be read through
in one year at the rate of ten or twelve verses a day.

2. The mind of fallen man is incapable of absorbing new
material every day. Especially when it comes to moral duties,
most of us need reminding far more than we need teaching.
So constant repetition of a few commands, a few promises
and a few facts, is more likely to influence choice and
character than an ever-changing kaleidoscope of brilliant
speeches and thrilling stories. John 20:31 suggests this reason
for the brevity of his Gospel:

> 'Many other signs therefore did Jesus in the presence of his
> disciples which are not written in this book: but these are
> written that you may believe that Jesus is the Christ, the
> Son of God, and that believing you may have life in his
> name.'

3. Another very important reason for short Gospels and
selected words has been discovered only by 20th century
research — that is, the vast multiplicity of languages. 5700
seems to be the latest figure. Even to translate Mark, the
shortest, into a tribal tongue takes (usually) not less than
four years; so just imagine what the Bible Society's task would
be like if every Gospel were as long as de Gaulle's biography,
i.e. twelve times the length of Matthew.

No! — God from the first intended that the Good News
should be preached and read in *every* language of the world so
that in the great multitude, which no man can number, shall
be some from all nations and kindreds and peoples and tongues.
And what do the world's leading linguistic experts say about
the Bible? 'The Bible is the most translatable and compre-
hensible religious book that has ever been written'! (Dr.
Eugene A. Nida, Research Coordinator of the United Bible
Societies, in *The Book of a Thousand Tongues*).

To many minds this seems strongly to confirm its divine

origin and inspiration; for if the sovereign Creator wished to reveal Himself to all mankind, He would surely do it in words intelligible to everyone everywhere, at all levels of education, in every culture and every century. And considering the communication problem sparked off at the Tower of Babel, the most vital truths of redemption had to be *condensed*.

CHAPTER THREE

Precis, Problems and Probabilism

'I wonder how much source-investigation in our studies of older literature seems solid only because those who knew the facts are dead and can't contradict it?'

C. S. Lewis, 'Fern-seed and Elephants'

Anyone who has tried to teach precis-writing will recognise the difficulty of reconstructing a whole text from (say) a dozen shortened forms of it. Each pupil will have different ideas about the relative importance or unimportance of particular phrases or paragraphs, what to include and what to leave out. For this reason it is easy to detect cheating in precis because the odds against two pupils writing even six identical consecutive words, are quite long.

Now modern scholars are fond of inventing 'explanations' of almost every difference between Matthew, Mark and Luke, where two or all of them record the same event or the same discourse. For various reasons, plausible or implausible, 'Matthew/Luke has changed/omitted/added this *probably* because . . .'. The following illustration may help us to see what a risky game it is to impute motives and assign reasons for literary transactions which took place nearly 2000 years ago in a distant country and alien culture, especially when it comes to putting a two-gallon speech into a pint bottle.

In 1978 the Reith Lectures were given by Dr. Edward Norman, Dean of Peterhouse. In the course of his first lecture, about 4000 words, he quoted Cardinal Mindzenty (approvingly) and Dr. Coggan (disapprovingly). Next morning both *The Times* and the *Daily Telegraph* printed a summary of his lecture in about 400 words. *The Times* summary was written by 'Our Religious Affairs Correspondent', the *Telegraph's* by Barry O'Brien.

Now let us imagine a Japanese Professor of Ancient European History in the year 3980 A.D. writing a book on *'Church and State in 20th Century Britain'*. He stumbles on these articles in *The Times* and *Telegraph* but has no means of telling their dates. He might plausibly comment on the Reigh Lecture as follows:

'A certain Barry O'Brien writing in the *Daily Telegraph* describes Edward Norman as a right-wing Anglican, but contradicts himself by also alleging that Norman quotes the Roman Catholic Cardinal Mindzenty as saying:

"I regard politics as a necessary evil in the life of a priest".

O'Brien is an Irish name and most Irishmen are Roman Catholics, so it is *probable* that O'Brien has used the lecture to introduce Catholic propaganda into the report. (Animosity between RC's and Protestants was running high in that decade because of the troubles in Ireland). This kind of addition would be considered dishonest in Japan but was quite common in 20th Century British journalism.

The Times carries a similar report by 'Our Religious Affairs Correspondent' who, under a cloak of anonymity, makes a direct attack on the Church of England. He alleges that Dr. Norman blames the Archbishop of Canterbury for asking this rhetorical question at a conference on Religious Education:

"Do we want to indoctrinate children into our own beliefs? God forbid!"

O'Brien *knows nothing* of this quotation, so it is *probably* a fiction invented by *The Times*. For who could believe that an archbishop would question the duty of Christians to teach their children Christianity? The thing is impossible. Dr. Coggan never said it and Dr. Norman never quoted it. Further research will no doubt throw more light on the motives of *The Times* correspondent, which may have been political.

However, there are two sentences common to O'Brien and *The Times*. We reproduce them here:

". . . the churches tag along, offering a religious gloss to precisely the same ideas. No one listens, for religion is no longer regarded as a guarantor of stability."

Probably this was copied: either O'Brien copied *The Times* or *The Times* copied O'Brien; or both copied the sentences from a now-lost source document which we will call Q. Q may have represented a collection of authentic sayings of the Dean of Peterhouse, and it is a pity we can get no nearer than this to the historical Edward Norman.'

To what purpose this farrago of nonsense? To demonstrate the confusion that results when an ignorant foreigner tries to make sense of a 4000-word lecture which has been reduced to 400 words by two independent reporters both of whom heard *exactly the same* words. Hypotheses are piled upon hypotheses until the researchers convince themselves they have done an excellent piece of sleuth work — when in fact they have only been chasing their own tails. Dr. Norman did quote *both* the Cardinal *and* the Archbishop, but O'Brien chose to repeat the former, *The Times* to quote the latter. Differences in wording were due to different emphasises, while the identical paragraph was due to both writers thinking it sufficiently important to quote verbatim in full. Obviously, O'Brien and *The Times* man did not see each other's precis until the Thursday morning when both papers were published simultaneously.

So it is, I believe, with the Gospels. Where they agree verbatim, it is nearly always in the words of Christ, which had sunk down deep in the apostles' memory and had been further riveted upon their minds by hearing each other preach for 20 years together in Jerusalem. Where they disagree, it is extremely unwise and unreasonable to impute ulterior motives for the 'omissions' and 'additions', since we know *less than 1%* of what they knew of Christ's words and deeds and contemporary events.

CHAPTER FOUR

Review of Reviewers

'While I respect the learning of the great Biblical critics, I am not yet persuaded that their judgment is equally to be respected.'

C. S. Lewis, 'Fern-seed and Elephants'

With modern critical scholars it is an article of faith that nothing written about the Gospels by Early Christians (100–200 A.D.) can be accepted at face value. Thus Nineham:

'The early Church was in the habit of assuming that all occurrences of a given name in the N.T. referred to a single individual, but when we remember that Mark (Marcus) was the commonest Latin name in the Roman Empire . . . we realise how precarious any assumption of identity is in this case.' (p. 39)

(For the early Church tradition about Mark's authorship, see pp. 135ff). So we are led to believe that the Mark of Papias was not our Mark, that the Matthew of Papias did not write our 'Matthew', and that John's Gospel was written by someone else of the same name.

How precarious is this assumption of non-identity may be illustrated by another little fantasy involving our hypothetical Japanese Professor, who, 2000 years hence, discovers two book reviews. The first is of a book entitled *Myths and Miracles* by David Watson, reviewed thus in *The Times Educational Supplement* for April 8th, 1977:

'. . . its arrangement makes it hard to read. Intended for schools, I think it would be *difficult to use* . . . there is in it some phoney-science . . . often the logic is false.'

The second review, apparently of a book bearing the same

title and written by someone of the same name, he finds in a quarterly magazine dated September 1977:

'David Watson's *Myths and Miracles* is lucid and entertaining, simple and profound . . . left casually in the classroom the book drew spontaneous interest from several 16-year-old biology students . . . they found the book *easy to read* straight through, challenging enough for deeper study. Teachers should find the book a treasure for both science and history classes . . .' (our italics)

Now, what will our Japanese Professor make of this apparent contradiction? Taking up his pen with an assurance worthy of a 20th Century critic, he writes:

'These books cannot be identical, though carrying the same title and apparently both written by "David Watson". It is impossible that one and the same book should evoke such absolutely contrary opinions as we find here expressed. But if the reviews refer to two different books, could two of the same title be written by two men of the same name in the same year? The answer is easy:

1. It is well established that there were in the 1970's *two* Christian writers named David Watson. In any case, the names David and Watson were so common in 20th Century Britain that any identification of one David Watson with another David Watson must remain very precarious. (Another was a soccer star!)

2. There was at this period an unusual interest in "myths" (cp. *The Myth of God Incarnate*) and miracles (cp. *Miracles* by C. S. Lewis), so quite possibly both David Watsons happened to hit on the same title.

3. *An Alternative possibility.*

Recently in Bonn a German book was discovered, dated 1975—85, entitled *Wundertaten und Mythen.* The first few pages are missing, so it is impossible to identify the author. But since British 20th Century theologians usually followed German scholars' opinions, it is most probable that one of the English books entitled *Myths and Miracles* is translated from the German. Then one "David Watson" was only a translater, and it is not clear who wrote the German original.'

ning and Reviewers* 13

(In fact the book reviewed in the *T.E.S.* is the *same* as that reviewed in the *Creation Research Society Quarterly*. It was published in 1976 and translated into German in 1978).

Conclusion: much learning added to much scepticism about traditional sources can lead to gross errors.

In passing we may note the somewhat eclectic use made of the Church historian Eusebius (325 A.D.). When A. W. Argyle wishes to debunk the idea that Matthew wrote the Gospel, he says:

> 'It is impossible to be sure what Papias meant (see p.112) or even whether his information is reliable. The fourth century historian Eusebius, who records Papias' statement, says that Papias was of very limited intelligence.'

What Argyle does *not* tell us is that this opinion of Eusebius has nothing whatever to do with Papias' reliability as a historian but refers only to Papias' extreme millennial views, of which Eusebius disapproved. In another passage Eusebius brackets together Polycarp, Papias and Ignatius as 'distinguished men' of the Church in Asia, and he certainly quotes Papias as a trustworthy authority for the circumstances surrounding the publication of Matthew's Gospel, Mark's and John's.

Even one translator (Loeb edition) of Eusebius seems to have been led astray by theological intimidation, perhaps, when he writes:

> 'Matthew *collected* the Oracles in the Hebrew language . . .'

The word should be translated 'composed'. We all know the difference, don't we? 'Mary, collect the papers in your class' means, pick up what other children have written. 'For homework I want you to write a composition on your visit to France', is another matter. Eusebius' word is used by him and by other Greek writers to mean 'compose' a narrative or poem. So Papias is not saying that Matthew collected scraps of paper written by others. He *is* saying that Matthew composed a narrative of the words and deeds of Jesus from his own personal experience of seeing and hearing Him.

CHAPTER FIVE

Did Matthew copy Mark?

'An illogical theology lands one in illogical situations; an ill-balanced theology issues in false emphasis and absurdity.'
Dorothy Sayers

'As most readers will know, when St. Matthew and St. Luke were writing they both had copies of Mark in front of them and incorporated almost the whole of it into their Gospels . . .'

The above sentence, which appears on p. 11 of Professor Nineham's *Commentary on Mark,* has been the theme song of most N.T. commentators for upwards of 50 years. However, I have yet to see any writer who makes a serious attempt to face the enormous problems posed by this theory . . . no one has begun to answer the question, how did Matthew persuade the whole Church throughout the Roman Empire to accept his *second*-hand version when there was already a *first*-hand version available (i.e. Mark's, from Peter)?

The following skit may help to pinpoint some of the difficulties.

Scene: A house in Jerusalem, 65 A.D. Matthew is sitting at a table. Enter Publius, a Christian from Rome.

Publius: Greetings, Matthew, from the brethren in Rome. I have brought you a copy of Peter's *Notes on the Life of Jesus,* which he called 'the gospel'. Mark, Barnabas' cousin, wrote it down at Peter's dictation.

Matthew: That's interesting. I must study it and see how it agrees with my memories.

Publius: Certainly. You take this copy and I'll have the other one copied by scribes for the church.

Next morning

Publius: Morning, Matthew. Have you had time to study Mark's Gospel?

Matthew: Yes, I spent three hours on it last night. Mark's done a pretty good job, considering that Peter's memory was always a bit shaky.

Publius: Are there any mistakes?

Matthew: Well, not exactly mistakes . . . but Peter seems to have left out some little extras that I always put into *my* sermons to impress people.

Publius: Such as?

Matthew: . . . for example in the Feeding of the 5000, I add 'besides women and children'. That makes the crowd at least twice as big, in people's imagination.
(Have you ever seen an Oriental crowd *without* women and children?)

Publius: Ah, that's clever!

A month later

Matthew: Publius, I've worked over Mark's Gospel and produced my own — better suited, I think, to the Christians here in Jerusalem. Would you like a copy to take with you back to Rome?

Publius: Well — er — yes, thank you, I suppose I would. But of course the Roman Christians will be used to Mark's by now. We had a good many copies made and most families will have one. Won't it look as though yours is sort of competing against his?

Matthew: Oh, I never thought of that . . .

Publius: Yes, and even here your church members have been copying Mark during this past month. There must be at least 50 copies around by now. They are delighted to have the story written down at last, backed by Peter's authority.

Matthew: That's awkward, isn't it?

Publius: Yes. If you have put 95% of his gospel into yours, people will say you want to supersede his.

Matthew: Well, in a way that might not be a bad thing. I've made some of the stories much easier to understand.

Publius: (coolly) Oh?

Matthew: Yes, for instance in the story of the Canaanite woman, I've made Jesus say, 'I was sent only to the lost sheep of the house of Israel', to explain His reluctance to help her. And I've completely re-written the Parable of the Sower.

Publius: Why?

Matthew: Mark puts singulars in the parable and plurals in the explanation. I've done just the opposite — put plurals in the parable and singulars in the explanation. A great improvement!

Publius: I'm sure you know best, Matthew. But it's puzzling for ordinary Christians like us. What difference does it make, anyway? Pardon my saying so, but I think these changes will cause a lot of confusion and may even split the Church!

Comment

What a ridiculous reconstruction!

Yes; but how else could the alleged 'copying' have been done? And there are other questions that demand an answer:

1. If Matthew had Mark in front of him, and knew that scores (at least) of copies had already been made, why should he bother to duplicate 95% of Mark's material? Why did he not limit his gospel to the additional material only (Sermon on the Mount, etc.) Why repeat in paler tones what had already been told with considerable vigour and colour?

2. Are we to believe that Matthew, or any Christian worthy of the name, would have wished to see his memoirs supersede those of Peter, the acknowledged leader of the Twelve? Or to have been content to introduce strife and argument which could so easily have been avoided by remaining silent on those parts of the story already covered by Mark?

We have now, I think, partly answered two questions:

1. Would any *apostle* have altered Mark's Gospel and incorporated it in his own memoirs?

2. Would any *Christian* have altered Mark in order to fit it into a patchwork of his own?

The answer to both these must surely be NO, unless we are prepared to affirm that the propagators of the purest morals the world has ever seen were not only cheats and consummate liars but also perfect *fools,* because their fanatical zeal won them only flogging, stoning, prison and death.

But a third question remains: would any *sane* man have altered the text so capriciously and uselessly as we in fact find it altered, if Matthew or Luke wrote their gospels with one eye on another gospel? How, for instance, can we explain the fact stated in our sketch — that Mark uses the singular 'it' for the seed in the Parable of the Sower, and the plural 'some people' in the explanation? — whereas Matthew does the opposite, speaking of seeds in the parable and 'he' in the explanation? (This distinction is obliterated in the *Good News Bible,* which actually conforms Matthew to Mark by putting the singular in vv. 4, 5, where the Greek has plural, and plural in vv. 19–23 where the Greek has singular.)

Either the author of Matthew must have been crazy to make such alterations, *or* he was deliberately trying to make his version appear as different as possible from Mark's, so that it might seem to be original.

An English Parallel

Here an illustration from Shakespeare may help. You remember Mark Antony's famous speech beginning: 'Friends, Romans, countrymen, lend me your ears . . .' Now suppose Ben Jonson (1573–1637) should have written another 'Julius Caesar' and included a similar speech for the same occasion, as follows:

> Friends, Romans, citizens, listen to me!
> I come to bury Julius, not to praise him.
> Men's evil deeds live on when they have died:
> The good they've done is all too soon forgotten.
> Thus let it be with Caesar . . .

What would we think of Ben Jonson (supposing it were proved that he wrote his 'Julius Caesar' *after* Shakespeare's)? Either he must have been crazy (to think he could get away

with it), *or* he was a dishonest playwright deliberately
plagiarizing and hoping *his* 'Julius Caesar' would rival and
eventually supersede Shakespeare's. Translated into English
the whole idea of such literary gymnastics looks extremely
foolish and indeed impossible. But let me assure non-Greek-
readers that no less absurdity is involved in the idea that
Matthew copied from Mark, chopping and changing word-
order, vocabulary, cases, prepositions, tenses and syntax *to no
purpose whatever,* since the underlying message was the same.
This is why Dr. Alford wrote:

> 'In no one case does any Evangelist borrow from another
> any considerable part of even a single narrative . . . It is
> inconceivable that any one writer borrowing from another
> (writer) matter of the very first importance, in good faith
> and with approval, should alter his diction so singularly and
> capriciously as we find the parallel texts of our Gospels
> "altered" . . . I do not see how any theory of mutual
> interdependence will leave to our three Evangelists their
> credit as able or truthworthy writers, *or even as honest
> men:* nor can I find any such theory borne out by the nature
> of the variations apparent in the text.'

(Dean Henry Alford D.D. was a Victorian scholar if not quite
the equal of Westcott and Lightfoot, yet certainly not far
behind them in learning and industry. His commentary on the
Greek New Testament, published in the 1850's, ran to about
2750 pages and is (to my knowledge) the only such English
commentary still in print (Moody Press, Chicago, 1958)).

CHAPTER SIX

Penny Farthing Theology?

'There used to be English scholars who were prepared to cut up Henry VI between half a dozen authors and assign his share to each. We don't do that now. Everywhere, except in theology, there has been a vigorous growth of scepticism about scepticism itself.'

C. S. Lewis, *'Fern-seed and Elephants'*

A recent issue of British stamps has reminded us of the evolution of the bicycle from early Victorian days. Most of us are thankful for the obvious superiority of the modern machine, and the tendency is to think of everything Victorian as quaint, old-fashioned and out of date. So when we find *modern* scholars putting forward new ideas about the Gospels, we naturally assume that the old ideas have been tried and found wanting and thrown on the scrap-heap like the old bone-shakers. Is this assumption valid?

In his book *Can we trust the New Testament?* Dr. J. A. T. Robinson writes: '. . . the answer to bad criticism was better criticism, as the great English biblical scholars like Lightfoot, Westcott and Hort saw.' It is pleasant to find such an accolade in such a book, and in a moment we shall take a look at this 'better criticism'. But first let us try to put the whole subject of modern scholarship into proper perspective.

To quote Robinson again: 'The winds of fashion (in theology) come and go, but the committed have their anchors and are content to ride out the storm.' That this storm is only a storm in a teacup will become evident when we look at the world as a whole and the growth of Christianity as a whole. Statistics show there are approximately 1000 million Christians, of whom about one million live in Britain. Of these church-goers probably not more than 5% i.e. 50,000 have ever read or are likely to read Dr. Robinson or Professor Nineham or any other critical scholar. At the same time we are told that no less than 55,000 people become Christians *every day;* and more than a million Bibles/N.T.'s/Gospels/Scripture portions are distributed *every day* in nearly 1700 different languages. All these Scriptures will carry the words of Christ as recorded in our Four Gospels, and they will be taught as the Word of God. From China to Peru, from Lapland to Lesotho, believers are being added to the Church. The idea that Oxford or Cambridge or London is still the theological centre of the universe is a delusion entertained by few non-Englishmen. 'He wist not that the Spirit of God had departed from him'. The candlestick has been removed, but the light shines on. Today the true successors of Lightfoot, Westcott and Hort are to be found elsewhere. Bible criticism influences only a minute proportion of the Church, probably not more than .1%: the vast majority of Christians are, *and always have been,* fundamentalists.

To return to the Cambridge trio. When J. B. Lightfoot died as Bishop of Durham in 1889, the Times wrote:

'The Church of England has been too soon deprived of one of the greatest minds by whom it has been served and adorned not only in this generation but in its whole history . . . He was at once one of the greatest theological scholars and an eminent Bishop.'

It is worth noting that Lightfoot and Westcott were first-class classical scholars in a day when classical scholarship was at its height, when knowledge of Greek was so common that it was used as a code by British Officers in the war of the Indian Mutiny. Westcott won four University prizes; Lightfoot was Senior Classic of his year and won the Chancellor's Medal. Some idea of what this means in terms of familiarity with the language of the N.T. can be gathered from this testimonial:

'I consider Mr. Westcott to have shown as complete and accurate a knowledge of the Greek and Latin languages as any candidate for classical honours ever obtained in the six years for which I have examined . . . He seemed to have read nearly every extract proposed. No shade of meaning

escaped his perspicacity; every particle and every syllable
of a compound received its due development. His composi-
tions in Greek and Latin were such as I have never seen
surpassed, and never hope I shall see . . . His papers contained traces of extensive and accurate researches into
ancient history, geography, and the manners and opinions
of those ages.'

(Rev. H. W. Beatson, examiner for the Classical Tripos 1839–
1849; quoted in the *Life of B. F. Westcott* by his son, 1903).
It may be doubted whether any 'modern scholar' has a
university record of equal distinction.

From the classics of ancient Greece and Rome, Lightfoot
and Westcott turned to the New Testament and the Fathers
of the Church, acquiring an encyclopaedic knowledge of their
writings. Westcott's *History of the Canon of the New Testament* and *Introduction to the Study of the Gospels* remained
standard works for half a century. What do they affirm? That
we have solid grounds for accepting, and no good grounds for
rejecting, the traditional belief in the authenticity and historical accuracy of the four Gospels. Westcott's books are out of
print today *not* because they have been proved erroneous but
because modern theological fashion decrees that early
Christian ideas about the Gospel are irrelevant, in fact 18
centuries of Christian thought and experience are largely
irrelevant. Now at last in the Space Age we have finally discovered how the Gospels were put together and what they
mean! We shall return later to this theme; but we must not
pass on before glancing at one of the greatest victories ever
won in the field of Christian apologetics — just 100 years ago.

Supernatural religion

It was in 1879 that the last edition appeared of a book whose
obituary notice we find in George Eden's *Life of Bishop J. B.
Lightfoot.* 'As an instance of the extraordinary influence of
J. B. Lightfoot's learning and authority among scholars may
be cited the effect of his essays published in the *Contemporary
Review* between 1874 and 1877, in criticism of an anonymous
book entitled *Supernatural Religion.* This apparently learned
book was 'an elaborate and systematic attack upon

Christianity', especially upon the credibility of the Christian
Fathers. The Dean of Lichfield writes:

> 'I remember a conversation with a well-known bookseller
> about Lightfoot's articles and he told me that they con-
> stituted the most remarkable phenomenon in the publishing
> trade that he had ever heard of. "When the book *Super-*
> *natural Religion* appeared", he said, "it had an extra-
> ordinary reception. It was emphatically praised by the
> reviewers, and its sale was so rapid that the publishers could
> hardly produce it fast enough to meet the demand. But
> before the series of Dr. Lightfoot's articles was even
> approaching completion, the book was already a glut in the
> second-hand market." '

These articles were reprinted as *Essays on 'Supernatural*
Religion' in 1889, and are worth their weight in gold. For the
benefit of those not lucky enough to possess a copy we shall
quote a few paragraphs:

1. 'As it will be my misfortune to dispute not a few proposi-
   tions which "most critics" are agreed in maintaining, it is
   somewhat reassuring to find that they are quite indifferent
   to the most elementary demands of grammar.' (One is
   reminded of the 'most scholars' so frequently referred to
   by Nineham).

2. 'If by an "apologist" is meant one who knows that he owes
   everything that is best and truest in himself to the teaching
   of Christianity — not the Christless Christianity which alone
   our author would spare, the works with the mainspring
   broken, but the Christianity of the apostles and Evangelists
   — who believes that its doctrines, its sanctions and its
   hopes are truths of the highest moment to the well-being of
   mankind and who, knowing and believing all this, is ready
   to use in its defence such abilities as he has, then a man
   may be proud to take even the lowest place among the ranks
   of "apologists".'

3. 'The rabbis were eminently learned, painstaking, minute;
   eminently ingenious also, and in a certain sense, eminently
   critical. In accumulating and assorting facts, the rabbis of
   Jewish exegesis might well bear comparison with the rabbis

of neologian criticism (i.e. 'modern scholars' as the phrase is used by Nineham). They reigned supreme in their own circles for a time . . . but their characteristic teaching, which they themselves would have regarded as their chief claim to immortality, has long since been consigned to oblivion . . . It was essentially unhistorical, and therefore it could not live. *The modern negative school of criticism seems to me to be equally perverse and unreal,* though in a different way; and therefore I anticipate for it the same fate.' (our italics)

4. 'I cannot pretend to be indifferent about the veracity of the records which profess to reveal Him whom I believe to be not only the very Truth, but the very Life.'

Another quotation is of more historical interest. In 1912 a learned Professor at Moscow remarked: 'It was your English scholars — Lightfoot, Westcott, Hort, Sanday and Armitage Robinson — who turned back and defeated the greatest modern threat to the Christian religion.'

CHAPTER SEVEN

Is Modern Scholarship Scholarly or Modern?

'Be sure that you go to the author to get at his meaning, not to find yours.'

John Ruskin

We shall take the second question first, and the answer seems to be: about as modern as Regent Street, or Mormonism; a lot older than the penny-farthing. For what today is called 'modern scholarship' is a direct descendant of what used to be called 'neologism' (= new ideas). The word was coined in the early 1800's to denote the rationalistic interpretation of the Bible which had crept into the German Church and was gradually spreading throughout Europe. A Bible Dictionary published in 1842 describes it as a system which 'tortures sacred scripture into seeming agreement with the fancies of human wisdom'. Two of its most powerful exponents were Alfred Loisy (1857–1940) in France and Julius Wellhausen (1844–1918) in Germany; and it is significant that DN refers to the former 9 times, to the latter 18 times. (But not once in the whole commentary does he mention Westcott or J. B. Lightfoot, whose writings did so much to counteract the influence of those sceptics). Let it be clearly understood, then, that the word 'modern' refers less to time than to a school of thought. There were modern scholars in the 1880's, and conservative scholars — like the Cambridge trio. There are modern scholars today, and conservative scholars. The moderns certainly *claim* that their views should supersede the old, traditional attitude to Scripture, so we shall now examine that claim with regard to 1. historical judgment; 2. textual interpretation.

Professor Nineham's comments on the story of Salome

'The story in Mark will be an account, written with a certain amount of literary freedom, of what was being darkly whispered in the bazaars of Palestine at the time . . . frequently inaccurate, and with something of the character of a fairy tale. In such an account it is idle to inquire too minutely into questions of historicity.'

But it is not idle to inquire whether Mark (or Peter) might not have had some more reliable source of information than a bazaar rumour. We find in Luke 8:3 that one of Christ's disciples was Joanna, wife of Chuza, Herod's steward; and in Acts 13:1 one of the teachers at Antioch was Manaen, foster-brother of Herod. So there were at least two Christians who had close contact with Herod's court and might easily have been eyewitnesses of the dancing episode, or received first-hand information about it.

Professor Nineham does not mention these facts, but repeats the fairy-tale theme in connection with the bringing-in of John the Baptist's head, because 'everything happens in quick succession'. On the other hand the conservative scholar Rev. A. Carr (CUP Matthew for Schools) informs us that at Machaerus Herod had a palace and a prison under the same roof; so John's head could indeed have been produced in little more time than it would have taken to serve the next course.

Another point on which Mr. Carr provides valuable information is the identity of Philip whose wife Herodias was stolen by Herod Antipas. Nineham assumes that this Philip is Philip the tetrarch of Ituraea, and that Mark got it wrong, because this Philip did not have a wife named Herodias. But Carr writes: 'she was wife of Herod's half-brother Philip — who was living in a private station (= held no public office) and *must not be confused with Philip the tetrarch.*'

Thirdly, Nineham accuses Mark of inaccuracy because Herod is called 'king' and speaks of his kingdom (v. 23). But Carr supports Mark by quoting the Greek historian Appian, who calls another tetrarch 'king'.

Fourthly, Nineham says it is incredible that a king's daughter should demean herself by dancing an 'oriental solo dance' in front of men. But a. traditional Jewish dancing is very far from being indecent; b. even if it was 'voluptuous', Carr informs us that the Roman satirist Horace complains that in his day *even highborn maidens* were learning the voluptuous dances of the East.

To sum up: Professor Nineham fails to mention five matters of historical fact each of which confirms the accuracy of Mark's account. Instead he contrives to throw doubt on the whole narrative by innuendo and ridicule, without producing one piece of real evidence that contradicts it. Moreover the story of Herod and Herodias contains nothing of the miraculous, nothing that we might not find in a secular history book. If this is the way he treats commonplace events, we may be pardoned for questioning his judgment of probabilities when dealing with the super-natural.

2. Now let's turn to Professor Nineham's comments on what he calls 'The Cure of the Deaf Mute' (Mark 7:32—37). Those who know the story may raise their eyebrows at the word 'mute', because Mark says the man 'had an impediment in his speech'. But Professor Nineham justifies his heading as follows:

> 'The phrase in v. 32 represents the exceedingly rare Greek adjective *mogilalos,* which means literally "speaking with difficulty" or "hardly able to speak". St. Mark *almost certainly* derived the word from the only other place where it occurs in the Greek Bible, Isaiah 35:6, where it translates a Hebrew word meaning "dumb". Then, seeing the miracle as the fulfilment of the prophecy, and influenced by the literal meaning of the Greek word, he took the miracle to consist in making the man speak *plainly. No doubt* the original story told of a deaf-*mute* who before the miracle could not speak at all.' (our italics)

To the present writer, such an interpretation must rank as a curiosity of Biblical criticism. The idea that Mark, having heard from Peter how Christ healed a dumb man, should change the story to fit a mistranslation, seems to me utterly fantastic. Let it be noted, first, that Mark himself says nothing about Isaiah 35. There is no 'that it might be fulfilled . . .'. No apologetic purpose is served by twisting the facts. Second, it is admitted by all that Mark wrote mainly for Gentile readers, most of them unfamiliar with the Greek

O.T. How many of them would have the remotest idea that
this miracle fulfilled Scripture? Third, Mark is very far from
being tied to the text of the LXX, as can be seen in his
quotation (direct from the Hebrew) in 4:12; Finally, and most
important, Nineham has made the all-too-common mistake of
academics — imagining that because a word is rare in sacred
literature, it must therefore be rare in everyday speech.

To test this I looked up 'stammer' in the *Oxford Book of
Quotations,* which contains about 350,000 words. The *only*
quotation in which this word occurs is William Cowper's
    'When this poor lisping stammering tongue . . .'
— but would it be true to say that 'stammer' is an 'exceedingly rare' word? Nineham seems to forget that Mark was a
human being who spoke Greek like a native, had probably read
scores of Greek books besides the LXX and had certainly seen
or heard of dozens of people who had the not-uncommon
affliction of stammering. Rarity of occurrence in classic
literature is no index whatever of a word's rarity in everyday
speech.

Conclusion

It may be argued that one should not generalise from a few
examples, but we believe that anyone who reads Professor
Nineham's commentary will soon see that these are far from
untypical. The author's *idee fixe* appears to be that every story
in the Gospel is as likely to be false as true. Every avenue is
explored that runs away from the obvious meaning of the
text; remote possibilities are upgraded to 'almost certainties';
references to 'the Greek' are often misleading, and 'almost all
scholars agree' is the knock-out blow to murmurs of dissent
from the layman.

It may be that, in the past, conservative scholars have
glossed over difficulties in the Gospels; but it is certain that
'modern scholars' have invented difficulties where none exist.
For 'scholarship' read 'scepticism'. Scepticism clouds the mind
no less than credulity. Scepticism warps historical judgment,
confuses linguistic analysis, and engenders hypotheses which,
if applied to any other type of literature, would be dismissed
as quite fantastic. One is reminded of J. B. Lightfoot's

comment on a German critic who tried to explain the names Syntyche and Euodias in Philippians: 'The learning of this curious pamphlet keeps pace with its absurdity' (SR p. 25).

CHAPTER EIGHT

What is 'Tradition'?

'. . . for this thing was not done in a corner.'
St. Paul (Acts 26:26)

The word carries a musty odour reminiscent of ancient cathedrals, Latin inscriptions and out-of-date hymn tunes. But closer inspection reveals an honourable pedigree. 'We celebrated Christmas in Timbuktu with the *traditional* turkey and plum puddings.' What does this mean? Surely that our feasting was *the same as it has always been as far back as anyone can remember*. Who first made up this menu, is of little importance. But the fact that it has been repeated year after year in millions of homes, is a very good indication, almost proof, that once upon a time this was *fixed* and the custom passed on from parents to children. A tradition, in fact, is history re-enacted. The same could be said of Guy Fawkes Night, which is imprinted on the minds of most English children far more than Waterloo or Trafalgar — simply because we *do* something to keep the memory alive.

So when Origen wrote that he had learned 'by tradition' that the first Gospel to be written was that according to Matthew, he certainly did not merely mean that he had once read it in a paragraph of old Bishop Papias. It means that wherever he travelled throughout the Roman Empire, to Rome or Greece, to Asia or Syria or Palestine, all Christians everywhere had been told by their parents, elders, pastors, teachers and bishops, *as far back as anyone could remember,* that Matthew wrote the first Gospel. No one had ever doubted or denied it.

In the 1830's a Professor Norton calculated that by 200 A.D. some 60,000 copies of the Gospels were in circulation

among at least 1000 Christian churches. So Matthew would
have been heard (on average) not less than 13 times a year by
not less than 1000 groups. 'Our third lesson is taken from the
Gospel according to St. Matthew . . .' (the first two lessons
being from the Law and the Prophets).

But suppose this does not satisfy someone. Suppose you
say, 'A tradition is something accepted without inquiry or
investigation. I want historical PROOF!'

What kind of proof?

Suppose we were to find in St. Catherine's Monastery on
Mount Sinai an ancient MS including this sentence (in Greek):

'I certify that I saw Matthew the apostle write a Greek
Gospel with his own hand.
                    (signed) James
                        Bishop in Jerusalem'

and suppose *that alone* were the evidence of Matthew's
authorship, who would believe it? Who will certify the
certificate? How can we check on a dead man's signature?

Far stronger, we believe, is the unanimous testimony of a
thousand Christian congregations scattered far and wide over
the ancient world, and continuing century after century. It is
a good test of truth that was framed by a later Christian,
St. Vincent of Lerins (450 A.D.):

Quod semper, quod abñique, quod ab omnibus creditum est
('that which has been believed always, everywhere, and by
everyone').

By this test it is as certain that Matthew wrote the first
Gospel as that Milton wrote 'Paradise Lost'. And this is what
Origen, Eusebius, and all the early Christians meant by
'tradition'.

ERRATA

Page 30 line 24 should read —
"Quod semper, quod ubique, quod ab omnibus
creditum est".

CHAPTER NINE

Professor Hunter and the Fourth Gospel

'St. John's is the only Gospel that claims to be the direct
report of an eye-witness. And to anyone accustomed to the
imaginative handling of documents, the internal evidence
bears out this claim.'

Dorothy Sayers

A. M. Hunter is not as radical as some critics. He appears to
believe in the Resurrection. He quotes Archbishop Temple's
faith in the Feeding of the 5000. But there are many disap-
pointments. He does not believe that the apostle John was
the author. He does not like the water-into-wine miracle at
Cana. In his view the most famous verse in the Bible, John
3:16, was not spoken by Jesus but made up by 'the evangelist', some Asiatic mystic, as was the discourse on the Bread of
Life in chapter 6. The healing of the nobleman's son is alleged
to be a garbled version of the healing of the centurion's
servant — in spite of the striking differences. In short he
denies the universal and unquestioned belief of the early
Church, that John the son of Zebedee in this book records
what he saw with his own eyes Jesus do, and what he heard
with his own ears Jesus say.

Now on what basis of superior learning does the Professor
make these bold claims, challenging the verdict of centuries?
Let us examine just *one* of his theories which contradict the
traditional view — in the story of Jesus walking on the water.
According to Hunter 'in John's account (6:16–21) no miracle
need be involved' because 'if John's Greek has the same
meaning as it has in 21:1, it should be rendered "by the sea",
i.e. on the shore or, at most, in the surf . . . Nor is it surprising that in the re-telling such an incident grew into a miracle.

For early Christian preachers the story must have made a
splendid illustration . . .'

When we turn to John 21:1 we find, sure enough, that the
same Greek word is used, thus: '. . . he manifested himself at
(epi) the Sea of Tiberias . . .' (6:19) '. . . they see Jesus
walking upon (epi) the sea and coming near the boat . . .'

But Hunter has forgotten an important though elementary
rule of Greek grammar: some prepositions, including epi, alter
their meaning when used with verbs of *motion.*

Now let's look at the verses again. In 21:1 the verb is
'manifested', obviously not a verb of motion, so the translation
'at' or 'by' the sea is correct. But in 6:19 the verb is 'walking',
implying movement, which is further emphasised by the added
'coming near to the boat'. So in 6:19 'epi' must mean 'over
the surface of' the sea, exactly as it does in Mark 6:48, 49.
(Hunter's explanation of their 'alarm' at seeing a figure
paddling by the shore is exceedingly lame, compared with the
obvious explanation, given by Mark, that they thought He was
a ghost). As a matter of fact we use our own word 'on' in
much the same way as the Greeks used 'epi'. a. 'I live at
Walton-*on*-Thames'; b. 'My son is rowing *on* the Thames
today'. We all understand that 'on' in a. means 'by the side
of', in b. it means 'on the surface of'.

Finally, note those fatal words: '. . . such an incident *grew
into a miracle.*' In the Gospel according to Hunter, the story
of the walking on the water in Matthew and Mark, with all
the attendant details (including Peter's attempt), is pure
fiction. Then why should not all miracles have grown out of
hazy recollections and preachers' exaggeration? This is the
logical deduction, and sixth formers (for whom chiefly the
book was written) will not be slow to make it.

Conclusion

In denying that John intended to record a miracle, Hunter contradicts the opinion of scores of scholars and commentators
(not a few of whom had Greek for their native tongue) and
introduces a disastrous principle of speculative negative
criticism. The whole weight of his objection to the traditional
view hinges upon his *ignorance of a point of Greek grammar.* It
is indeed a tragedy that such a mistake should be made by
such a man in such a book, whose readers have no means of
checking on the original.

CHAPTER TEN

The Case of the Rustling Leopard

*'The canon "If miraculous, unhistorical" is one they bring
to the study of the texts, not one they have learned from
it.'*

C. S. Lewis, *'Fern-seed and Elephants'*

Recently I came across an interesting passage on which budding
critics might test their ingenuity. Here are two versions of
what appear to be one story. The puzzle is to detect:

1. Which was written first.
2. Whether the same writer wrote both versions.
3. Why he (or the other writer) changed the words as he
did.
4. Whether the story is true.

Version A

'Hearing him (the leopard) was the strangest experience I have
ever had. I never heard any animal's body before and cannot
in any way account for the sound. It was loud enough to be
heard at 30 yards and was exactly like a woman walking in a
stiff silk dress. The field had lately been planted with wheat
and there was not a leaf or a blade of grass in it. No, the sound
did not come from his feet but from his body.'

Version B

'. . . the sound he made when walking I could not then, nor
can I now account for; it was like the soft rustle of a woman's
silk dress, and could not be explained by stubble in the field
— for there was none — or by the loose straw lying about.'

Using familiar methods, a modern scholar might comment:
'The precise historical basis of this story, whatever it may have

been, is now irrecoverable. Everyone knows that leopards do not rustle when they walk, so we must exercise our imagination to discern the purpose of this legend. Most scholars agree that the tale was told to satisfy the needs of simple Indian villagers who idolised Corbett and liked to imagine that the leopard he shot was possessed of supernatural powers. There are also references in the Hindu Scriptures to gods becoming incarnate in animals, and doubtless this idea influenced the villagers' thinking.

'Version B was clearly written first. Version A heightens the sense of miracle by adding corroborative epithets —

loud enough to be heard at 30 yards . . .
exactly like a woman . . .
stiff silk dress . . .

so was probably written afterwards to lend verisimilitude to an otherwise bald and unconvincing narrative. This is typical of the way a legend builds up over the years when often repeated and embellished to please an ingenuous audience.'

In fact both accounts were written by Jim Corbett, version A in a letter to the *Pioneer* in 1925, version B in his book *The Man-Eaters of Kumaon* 22 years later — the same man recalling the same facts as he really experienced them, but using a slightly different vocabulary because of the elasticity of the human mind. The reconstruction of our Corbett-scholar is thus seen to be a total myth-construction.

Lest any should think that the above is a 'straw-man' argument, let me quote a. from a footnote in Professor Nineham's introduction:

'The formulation of the tradition regarding Jesus was a work of enthusiasm . . . it was in this enthusiasm that the preacher or teacher could not be restrained from *adding his own comment* to the narrative' (H. A. Guy).

b. Nineham p.444 (on Mark 15:5)
'. . . it is probable that Mark's description is *imaginative;* he picturesquely describes what he believes happened.'

So pages and pages of modern commentaries are filled with myth-constructions no less chimerical than the Corbett-myth. In the Greek text there is not one jot or tittle of evidence that any Evangelist or copyist added imaginative touches to any story. The similarities are there because eyewitnesses saw the same things happen; the differences because eyewitnesses used different words to describe those same events (or the *different* experiences of disciples after the Resurrection).

And in all four Gospels, adjectives and adverbs — the stock in trade of preachers — are conspicuously absent.

We dare to suggest that it is the critics' imaginative faculty, rather than the Evangelists', that has been allowed too much freedom. Possibly with half an eye on pleasing *their* 'ingenous audience', they picturesquely describe what they believe happened in the composition of the Gospel. (our italics throughout)

There is another lesson we can learn from the Introduction to Jim Corbett's *India*. R. E. Hawkins writes:

'As a man he inspired complete confidence.'

This is what modernist scholars seem to overlook. People read any fiction for entertainment, but they will not forsake the time-honoured customs and religion of their ancestors and embark on a totally new way of life *unless* they have complete confidence in the integrity of their new teacher. Behind the universal and unwavering acceptance of the Gospels throughout the early Church, from Gaul to Alexandria, from Carthage to the Black Sea, stands the unchallenged integrity of the apostles as men who would never tell a lie. People who knew Jim Corbett best, believed him best; and so it must have been with Matthew and John, Peter and Luke. No one has ever produced a scintilla of evidence that the apostles preached in order to gain a following, or earn a living, or to confound the Jews, or write a best-seller. All the evidence points the other way, that they were absolutely disinterested, fearless, loving and truthful. No others could have turned the world upside down, as they did.

So the answer to the question: Are the Gospels true? is — yes, they must be, because each Evangelist 'as a man, inspired complete confidence' in those who knew him best. We cannot explain the story of the rustling leopard, but we can believe the story-teller. We cannot explain Christ's miracles, but we have every reason to believe that the apostles, like Corbett, told the truth.

Reporters or artists?

The idea that a liberty in story-telling is allowed in the
pulpit which would be denied to an historian in the lecture-
hall, may be fashionable in Cambridge but is utterly at
variance with the Book of Acts — our only reliable source of
information about preaching in the early Church. Nothing
there is said by Stephen, Peter or Paul except the plain
truth. Peter made very modest claims for his Master when he
told Cornelius that Jesus 'went about doing good'. A modern
journalist would say He went about doing stupendous miracles.
We find no two levels of talking or writing, no fact and fancy
intermingled. The very idea of such mis-mating of light with
darkness is, I may say, abhorrent to a sensitive Christian
conscience. Monkish inventions and religious romance belong
to a later age, as will soon be perceived by anyone who
studies the Apocryphal N.T. (OUP) edited by M. R. James.
(Dr. Montagu Rhodes James, still famous as a ghost-story
writer, was one of the most learned men of his generation:
Provost of King's, Cambridge, then of Eton College). He
writes:

> 'The Apocryphal Gospels and Acts . . . do not achieve
> either of the two principal purposes for which they were
> written, the instilling of true religion and the conveyance
> of true history . . . Among the prayers and discourses of
> the apostles in the spurious Acts, some utterances may be
> found which are remarkable and even beautiful: not a few
> of the stories are notable and imaginative. But the authors
> do not speak with the voices of Paul or of John, or with
> the quiet simplicity of the first three Gospels . . . In short,
> the result of anything like an attentive study of the
> literature, in bulk and in detail, is an added respect for the
> sense of the Church Catholic, and *for the wisdom of the
> scholars of Alexandria, Antioch and Rome*[1]: assuredly in
> this case they were tried money-changers, who proved all
> things and held fast that which was good.' (our italics)

In other words this very learned scholar, who spent half a
life-time studying writings which attribute to Jesus words that

---

1. See pp.151–8.

He never spoke, concludes that men like Clement and Origen were absolutely right in accepting our Four Gospels as true history and rejecting all others. It is certain that, were he alive today, he would repudiate the hypothesis that the authors of Matthew, Mark, Luke and John were creative and imaginative artists, weaving together strands of narrative and discourse which may or may not represent what Jesus actually said and did.

Finally, Bishop Westcott (as quoted by G. F. Maclear, D.D. in the Cambridge Bible for Schools, St. Mark, 1883):

> 'In substance and style and treatment, the Gospel of Mark is essentially a transcript from life. The course and issue of facts are imaged in it with the clearest outline. If all other arguments against the mythic origin of the Evangelic narratives were wanting, *this vivid and simple record,* stamped with the most distinct impression of independence and originality, totally unconnected with the symbolism of the Old Dispensation, totally independent of the deeper reasoning of the New, *would be sufficient to refute a theory subversive of all history.*' (our italics)

CHAPTER ELEVEN

The Wicked Husbandmen

'In modern memoirs written by real people about another real person we should expect just that sort of diversity which we find in the Gospels.'

Dorothy Sayers

One of the most important facts overlooked by modern critical scholars is the fact that Jesus was a *preacher,* not a writer. There is a vast difference between the two accomplishments. In recent years David Kossof has shown us how to make O.T. stories live, and he does so (of course) by *expanding* them and adding a lot of interesting detail which a writer might well leave out in order to save space. Now, Dr. Robinson (CWTNT) has selected the Parable of the Wicked Husbandmen to demonstrate how a story 'develops' from one Gospel to another. By paring it down, or (to change the metaphor) by unwrapping it and discarding all the trimmings, he manages to reduce it to 116 words which *he* believes is as near as we can get to what Jesus actually said.

Will you please now take up your Bible and time yourself reading the first 11 verses of Mark chapter 12. How long did it take you? It took me 65 seconds. But can we really imagine that Jesus, preaching in the Temple from early dawn, spent only *one minute* out of a whole day to tell this parable?

We read that 'the people all hung upon Him, listening', and 'the common people heard Him gladly'. Now ordinary people do not get up early in the morning (Luke 21:38) to hear a preacher unless he is very interesting, persuasive, and a great story-teller. And the whole art of story-telling, as Chaucer might have taught us, is suspense . . . which requires *spinning out* a tale, introducing diversions and delays, so that the audience becomes restive in their eagerness to hear the end. But what kills a story dead as a doornail? Why, to be told the end within 65 seconds of the beginning! Which is what the critics would have us believe Jesus did, not once or twice but twenty times, if He told the parables exactly as they are written, without adding any colourful background.

Luke says this Parable of the Wicked Tenants made the chief priests so angry that they wanted to arrest Him then and there. Is it not much more probable that it was told with considerable elaboration and detail — there may have been some heckling, or at least question and answer and then what we have recorded in Matthew, Mark and Luke is three independent precis as remembered by three ear-witnesses.

Independent, because how otherwise can we account for the fact that the opening sentence of each version is totally different from the opening sentence of the other two, thus:

Matthew: Man there was householder who planted vineyard
Mark: Vineyard man planted and placed around hedge
Luke: Man planted vineyard

Matthew: and hedge to it placed around and dug in it
Mark: And dug winepress (*different* word from Matthew's)

These are just the sort of variations one would expect from three independent reporters, bearing in mind that the order of words in Greek is far more variable than in English. Luke omits all mention of the hedge and winepress, but only (we suggest) because they are not strictly pertinent to the main point of the story. On any hypothesis of mutual dependence these differences are quite inexplicable.

We therefore conclude: Dr. Robinson's theory that the 'ipsissima verba' of Jesus are to be found in the shortest version of the parable, is the exact opposite of the truth. From all that we know of preaching and preachers, it is far more likely that Jesus' actual words included very much more than has been recorded. What the Evangelists have given us is the distilled quintessence of divine truth.

CHAPTER TWELVE

A Golfing Legend

'We need not imagine that the appearance of the same story in different contexts argues any inaccuracy or contradictions, or that the version of one Evangelist is more authentic than that of another.'

Dorothy Sayers

We reproduce two reports on the Bob Hope Desert Classic, 1979.

Puzzle: to discover the relationship between them.

Reporter M. '. . . third prize of £1350 went to Mike Hayes with a 66. Mahaffey came under considerable pressure throughout the day. Lee Trevino, determined and without any heroics, stayed very much in contention. Throughout all this Mahaffey stood firm. Trevino, almost gripping Mahaffey's shoulder, sank a 10-foot putt at the 18th for a birdie to finish with a 69 . . . From 80 yards could Mahaffey get down with a pitch and putt to win outright? His wedge finished 15 ft. short of the hole. No problem. Mahaffey sent his putt into the middle of the hole for victory.'

Reporter T. 'John Mahaffey, facing up to a 15 ft. putt on the last green, told himself: "After all, you're the PGA champion and World Cup winner. This is just another putt. Knock it in." He did just that, and his final round of 69 gave him the £27,000 first prize by one stroke over Lee Trevino. The Mexican, who had also birdied the 18th a few minutes before, threw down the apple he was munching and — to his eternal credit — laughed and cheered like everyone else. Trevino's 69 won him £15,000 while young Mark Hayes's 66 took the third prize of £9,350.'

Comment by a 'modern scholar'

'It is clear that Reporter T has a distinct bias in favour of Trevino, whom he depicts as an exceptionally good loser, and against Mahaffey, who is depicted as a boastful winner. Reporter M *knows nothing*[1] of Mahaffey talking to himself, nor of Trevino laughing at his opponent's victory. He depicts the championship as a grim struggle . . . note the words "pressure", "determined", "contention" etc. Again, Reporter M is probably nearer the truth when he gives the 3rd prize as £1350. If Reporter T was a Mexican it would be natural for him to exaggerate the prize-money of his hero Trevino; then the first and third prizes too would have to be enhanced to make the story plausible . . . Exactly what was spoken on and around the 18th green at Palm Springs will never be known, but these differing reports show how the tradition of a golfing victory could grow into a legend.'

ANSWER. Reporter M stands for Monday and Reporter T for Tuesday. Both reports were written by the *same* man, Alex Lancaster, and printed in the Daily Telegraph respectively on Monday, January 15th and Tuesday, January 16th, 1979. The figure £1350 was evidently a misprint, £9350 is correct.

* * *

Perhaps this little diversion will help us to see that spinning hypotheses as to why one writer differs from another in reporting the same event, is good clean fun and a harmless pastime, but more than likely to produce results wholly at variance with truth.

Why does Matthew omit, and Mark include (7:27), the sentence 'Let the children first be fed . . .' in the story of the Canaanite Woman? According to Professor Nineham, Matthew does not picture Jesus as envisaging a later mission to the Gentiles; Mark does. But what about Matthew 28:19 —

---

1. Compare DN p.444: 'The Marcan tradition clearly *knew nothing* of any sealing or guarding of the tomb . . .' J. B. Lightfoot writes (SR p.33) 'The argument from silence is courageously and extensively applied throughout these volumes (*Supernatural Religion*) . . . "knows nothing" is substituted for "says nothing" as if the two were convertible terms.

'disciple all the nations'? Ah, that's easy — quote Vincent
Taylor: 'Mark 16:15 is *no more than* Matthew 28:18ff an
actual saying of Jesus'. VT locutus est, causa finita est!
(Vincent Taylor has spoken: the case has been decided). But
then why does *Mark* include 'Let the children first be fed . . .'?
Answer: he didn't! Who says so? 'Most commentators'.

In other words, starting from the presupposition that Jesus
never talked about a world-mission to Gentiles, 'modern
scholars' or 'most commentators' systematically eradicate[1] all
verses in the Gospel which contradict their theory . . . and
then come up triumphantly with, 'You see, I was right!'.

In 1886 J. B. Lightfoot wrote about the author of *Supernatural Religion:*

'He imagines that, as long as he does not advance anything
which is demonstrably impossible, he may pile one improbability upon another without endangering the stability of
his edifice.'

Perhaps the old man is yet alive, in his spiritual great-grand-
children — modern scholars.

A good example of the 'Mark says nothing = Mark knows
nothing' fallacy is provided by Eusebius himself, who quotes
Matthew 28:19 as 'Go and make disciples of all the nations
in My name'. This worries Professor Kirsopp Lake, who finds
it necessary to add a footnote (Loeb Library Vol. I p. 299):

'This is the form in which Eusebius usually quotes Matthew
28:19, omitting the reference to baptism. It cannot be
accidental, but there are no MSS of the NT with this text
i.e. omitting the second half of the verse). Some think that
Eusebian text is the earlier form, some that Eusebius wished
to keep secret the formula of baptism.'

But why on earth should an historian quote more of a verse
than is absolutely necessary for his purpose, and his purpose
in this passage is perfectly clear — to explain why the
apostles finally left Jerusalem. We have no more reason to
assume he did not know the baptismal formula than we would

---

1. Or nearly all. DN has missed Matthew 8:11 ('many shall come from
   the east and the west . . .'). Although he refers to it five times, he
   never comments on its obvious relevance to Gentile evangelisation.

for thinking that Dr. Martyn Lloyd Jones or John Stott do not know it because they might choose to preach on 'Go, make disciples of all nations'. Writing for those who might be expected to possess a copy of Matthew's Gospel, Eusebius simply reminds his readers of some few words of the Lord which would have been specially in the Apostles' minds as they left the seat of Judaism and ventured forth to Gentile lands. Baptisms there had been a-plenty throughout the past 20 years: it was the *new* challenge of *un*familiar people that faced them. So Eusebius rightly stressed that fact and that fact alone.

On exactly the same principle each writer stresses those *particular* things that seem to him important enough to be included in the very narrow limits of his Gospel (see chapter 2). To assume ignorance from silence is to misunderstand both the historian and the Evangelist.

CHAPTER THIRTEEN

Doublets

It is a cardinal principle of modern critics that most incidents in the Gospels that look somewhat similar are the *same* incident retailed in a garbled manner by different 'traditions'. Perhaps the most notorious of these allegations is that which identifies the Feeding of the Five Thousand with that of the Four Thousand. A modern parallel may help to show how precarious is this identification. We shall again take a leaf out of a History of Europe written by a Japanese Professor in 3900 A.D.:

'The alleged sinking of the *Lusitania* in May 1915 was clearly a romance invented by Winston S. Churchill, First Lord of the Admiralty, in order to denigrate the Germans and bring America into the war. Only a naive literalist would imagine that there could be two separate sinkings of two giant liners within three years. This will become apparent if we set out the stories in parallel, thus:

Titanic (sunk April 1912)	**Lusitania** (May 1915)
luxury transatlantic liner	luxury transatlantic liner
four funnels	four funnels
speed 23 knots	speed 23 knots
warnings ignored (ice)	warnings ignored (German Embassy)
carrying many wealthy Americans	carrying many wealthy Americans
struck iceberg	struck by torpedo
in mid-Atlantic — (a)	near coast of Ireland
not enough lifeboats	inadequate life-saving equipment

Titanic—*continued*	**Lusitania**—*continued*
sank in 4 hours — (b)	sank in 8 minutes
1503 lost	1198 lost
703 saved	761 saved

'The differences can easily be explained. a. The disaster
was supposed to have taken place near Ireland so that no
American ships or reporters could have witnessed it. b. The
time taken for the Lusitania to sink was shortened to 8
minutes to emphasise the ferocity of the Huns' attack. As
so often, history is seen to be the propaganda of the victors.'

What our clever Japanese Professor has forgotten is that
700 survivors of the Titanic *lived to tell the tale*. Would they
have kept silent when another story was published so similar
to their own, but obviously a fake? I think not. And what
clever English/German Professors forget when they conspire
to call the Feeding of the Four Thousand a 'doublet' is that
there were thousands of 'survivors', at least in Palestine, who
had actually witnessed the Feeding of the Five Thousand, or
heard about it from participants. For Matthew to publish his
account of the Four Thousand with such people as his potential
readership, would be to invite derision and repudiation of the
whole Gospel — *unless it was true.*[1] A very important point
is made by the Athenian apologist Quadratus (130 A.D.):

'The works of our Saviour were ever present; for they were
real: being the men who were healed: the men who were
raised from the dead: who were not only seen at the moment
when the miracles were wrought, but also (were continually
seen like other men) being ever present; and that not only
while the Saviour sojourned on earth but also after his
departure for a considerable time, so that some of them
survived even to our times (i.e. the 2nd century)'.

The fact is that history *does* repeat itself; and in any other
discipline except theology a scholar who made a habit of
squeezing two similar stories into one would be laughed out
of court. Was Winston Churchill, First Lord once, or twice?

1. For further study please refer to R. C. Trench's *Notes on the Miracles*
   (Baker Book House, Grand Rapids, Michigan). Highly recommended.

Did Julius Caesar invade Britain once, or twice? He himself is our only original authority for the notion that it was twice: yet no historian doubts that Caesar wrote the truth.

Augustine remarks that if Matthew had recorded the Five Thousand miracle only, and Mark the Four Thousand only, many cavillers would have argued there was only *one* miracle for (say) 4500! But in fact both Evangelists record both miracles, which makes assurance doubly sure that both really happened.

CHAPTER FOURTEEN

Squealerisms

'Neither in the content nor in the style of these texts is there anything redolent of fake or hysteria. Quite the reverse. The gospel-writers . . . invariably show the detachment of the objective reporter.'
V. Messori, Jesus Hypotheses, 1976

Readers of *Animal Farm* will remember the cunning antics of Squealer, who secretly changed the original wording of the Seven Commandments, one by one, to suit the downward trend in pig-morality and pig-manners. 'No animal shall kill another animal' became 'No animal shall kill another animal *without cause*'; 'no animal shall drink alcohol' became 'no animal shall drink alcohol *to excess*', etc. etc., until the original Seven became hardly recognisable. Now, according to modern scholars, some such process went on in early Christian editorial offices to suit the 'broadening' trend in church-morality and church-manners; and 'modern scholarship' has done a brilliant job of removing the later layers of paint, so to speak, and restoring to us the 'original' words of Jesus (or others). In A. W. Argyle's *Commentary on Matthew* (CUP) I have counted 20 such 'squealerisms', i.e. alleged attempts by 'Matthew' to whitewash the apostles or adapt Christ's teaching by editorial additions or subtractions. These include changing the grounds of divorce (p. 51), adding 'Our' to the Lord's Prayer (i.e. 'Our Father') (p. 56), adding 'women and children' to the Five Thousand to magnify the miracle (p. 113), inventing Peter's walking on the water ('Mark appears to *know nothing* of this adventure' p. 116), and blaming James' and John's mother for their ambition 'in order to spare the apostles, Matthew shifts the responsibility' p. 153. What a gallant Christian gentleman to cast gratuitous aspersions on a woman!)

The layman who has hitherto fondly imagined that he was reading *facts* in the Gospel, now discovers that not a little of it is, after all, *fiction*; and moreover fiction masquerading as fact. It was not, then, Matilda, but Matthew, who

'. . . told such awful lies
It makes one gasp and stretch one's eyes.'

The stream is polluted at source, apparently; for, if we are to believe Dr. J. A. T. Robinson (and he gives excellent reasons), 'Matthew' must have been written not more than 40 years after the Resurrection.

Do we realise what the critics are saying? They affirm that the religion which more than any other emphasises *truthfulness* as an absolute requirement ('Thou desirest truth in the inward parts', Psalm 51), which stigmatizes the devil as the Father of lies, and damns all liars to perdition (Revelation 22) — *this* religion was propagated by deceivers who in return for their 'lies' gained nothing for themselves but persecution, torture and death. Robinson, Nineham and Argyle fail nowhere so conspicuously as in their extraordinary blindness to this moral issue. They are in fact making St. John and St. Matthew, if not Mark and Luke, into Squealers. ('Some of the animals heard this with a certain bewilderment, but Squealer was soon able to convince them that their memories had been at fault', AF p. 83). They also claim that the 'truth' about Gospel mythology has been discovered only in the last 150 years, so 60 generations were at least partly deceived by the fake pictures of Christ which have now been restored to their pristine splendour. But most Christians will agree with C. S. Lewis[1] that it is 'quite incredible that we should have had to wait nearly 2000 years to be told by a theologian . . . that what the Church has always regarded as a miracle was, in fact, a parable!' (referring to the miracle at Cana; but the remark is applicable to all such modern 'reconstructions').

1. Fern Seed and Elephants.

CHAPTER FIFTEEN

Luke will be laughing

'. . . *there is no more searching test of a theology than to submit it to dramatic handling; nothing so glaringly exposes inconsistencies . . . as to put it upon the stage and allow it to speak for itself.*'

Dorothy Sayers

One temptation which critics find hard to resist is that of imputing to the Evangelists motives which, it may fairly be said, would never have entered the mind of ordinary Christians. In this chapter we shall look at the alleged reasons for two 'omissions' and one 'transposition' by Luke. But first, a recent publication may teach us how rash it is to attribute motives where we really know nothing of the author's mind. We quote from David Holloway's review of *The Victorian Public School* (Gill & Macmillan) in the *Daily Telegraph,* May 9, 1976:

'One of the most interesting papers is Patrick Scott's detective work about the writing of Thomas Hughes's *Tom Brown's Schooldays.* It is *usually assumed* that the change in tone between the naturalistic first half (football, fights and Flashman) was written before the death of Hughes's daughter. The more moralistic second half (Arthur and the cricket match) is *conjectured* to be the product of his mourning.

'Mr. Scott, by delving into the publishers' papers, finds that *the reverse is true.* The first half of the book was lost by accident and re-written after the second half was in the hands of the printers. Indeed Hughes left a synopsis showing that the novel, as it appeared, was exactly as he had conceived it before his daughter's death.' (our italics)

What a pity that we cannot delve into Dr. Luke's papers. If we could, I believe that many of the critics' *usual assumptions* and *conjectures* would turn out to be *the reverse of true*. For if literary critics speaking the same language and inheriting the same culture as their author's can make such mistakes only 100 years later, how much more are they likely to err when trying to analyse the motives of a man who wrote in an alien tongue and a distant land 19 centuries ago.

Now for examples:

1. Luke omits the Cursing of the Fig Tree *probably because he regarded it as unedifying* and also because he had already recorded the parable of the fruitless fig tree' (AWA, Matthew, p. 159).

First, it may be worth pointing out that he who thinks of Luke's Gospel as all sweetness and light, angels and shepherds, the Good Samaritan and the Prodigal Son, needs to look again. Luke is the only Evangelist who uses the word 'vengeance' (three times); and only Luke records 'there shall be *wrath* upon this people' (21:23). His gospel also includes the only close-up picture we have of Hell (Rich Man and Lazarus), and he alone has the four 'Woes' to balance the four beatitudes (6:20–26). So it hardly seems probable that Luke would have refused to include Christ's solemn words to the barren fig tree on the grounds that they were 'unedifying'. Furthermore we can see in the conversion of Zacchaeus a good illustration in real life of the parable of the Lost Son, noting especially the similarity of 19:19 to 15:31 ('. . . to seek and to save that which was lost.' '. . . he was lost, and is found.'). So there is no reason why Luke should not have included the Cursing of the Fig Tree as another illustration in real life of another parable — that of the Barren Fig Tree (13:6–9).

2. Christ's lament over Jerusalem.

AWA's comment (p. 178); 'Luke places the present passage before the entry (into Jerusalem) so that the words are a prediction of it' (i.e. of His entry).

We shall dramatise this 'transposition' and see whether it makes sense.

Scene: Paul's hired house in Rome, 62 A.D.

Luke: Paul, I'm just putting the final touches to my gospel. I see Matthew puts Jesus' lament over Jerusalem after He was inside the city walls, two or three days *after* the crowd had shouted 'Blessed is he that comes in the name of the Lord!' Then what did he mean by predicting they would say it again?

Paul: Not sure, old boy. Something to do with the second coming, perhaps.

Luke: Well, I think it'll be better to push it back a few pages, then His words will sound like a prophecy that was fulfilled when He *did* enter Jerusalem.

Paul: Good idea. All's fair in love and war, and we really do have a war on to convince these stubborn Jews that Jesus could foresee the future.
(*later*) Luke, I've read through your version of Jesus' lament. Why did you change Matthew's *episunaxai* (= to gather together) to *episunagagein* (= to gather together)? also 'her' into 'her own', and 'chickens' into 'brood'? (see the RV of 1881 which makes an accurate distinction between these words).

Luke: Tactics, my dear Paul, tactics! When people compare my passage with Matthew's it will look more plausible if *some* words are different. They'll think that Jesus used slightly different wording on two separate occasions. Of course it won't be true, but what does that matter as long as they believe?

Comment

Anyone who thinks that Christian men could talk and act like this is welcome to his opinion, but let him not pretend this is the common view of Christendom. To most of us it betrays a revolting duplicity unthinkable in an ordinary Christian, let alone in apostles of Jesus Christ. The only theory that fits the facts is that Jesus *did* speak roughly the same words at least twice (perhaps twenty times) on different occasions; and this could well account for the minute variations which are reproduced only in the AV and RV. (Unfortunately both the RSV and the Good News Bible render the two passages word for word the same, although in the Greek

five words are different. Thus is perpetuated the myth that
Luke copied from Matthew or Q or vice versa, and young
Christians miss the infinite variety of the Bible).

The rewards of service

We now revert to the Pelican Commentary on Mark 10:29:

> 'There is no man that has left house, or brothers or sisters
> or mother or father, or children or lands, for My sake and
> for the gospel's sake, but he shall receive a hundredfold
> now in this time, houses and brothers and sisters and
> mothers, and children and lands, with persecutions; and in
> the world to come eternal life.'

Professor Nineham's comment: 1. '. . . the repetition of the
list seems *intolerably flat* and already appeared so to St.
Matthew and St. Luke, who both omit it.' (our italics)

2. 'The absence of "wife" from the list may well be
significant.' (Luke *does* include 'wife' in his list.)

We now present two scenes based upon these comments. It
is for the reader to judge whether they are likely ever to
have happened.

A house in Rome

Scene I: The Gospel Publication Committee are seated round
a table.

Aquila: Now that Mark's gone to Egypt, it's time we published his Gospel. But I'm hesitant about one or two points.

Andronicus: Which?

Aquila: Well, in 10.39 he suggests it may be necessary to
leave one's *wife* behind when preaching the gospel. But
Priscilla has come with me in all my travels, and she intends
to continue!

Urbanus: No harm in that, I'm sure. Yes, the words as they
stand might be misleading to our people. Why not delete
'wife' from the list?

Aquila: An excellent idea. All in favour?

Philologus: Not so fast, Aquila. I think we should stick to what Peter told Mark. After all, Peter heard the Lord, we didn't.

Aquila: Well, let's put it to the vote with a show of hands. Those in favour of deleting 'wife'. Thank you. Sorry, Phil, your objection is overruled. Amendment carried by ten votes to one.

Prison in Caesarea

Scene 2: Luke and Paul are seated at a table, Luke writing and Paul reading Mark's Gospel aloud to him.

Paul: '. . . there is no one who has left house or brothers or sisters or mother or father or children or lands, for my sake and for the gospel, who will not receive a hundredfold . . .'

Luke: What about 'wife'? I'm sure I heard Andrew quote the Lord as including 'wife' in the list.

Paul: Well, it's not here. Perhaps Peter left it out, being a married man. And I believe Aquila had a hand in the publication. He never goes anywhere without Priscilla!

Luke: I'm going to put in 'wife' anyway. You and I as bachelors know how much more work we get done without the apron strings.

Paul: (continues reading) '. . . now in this time, houses and brothers and sisters and mothers and children and lands, with persecutions . . .'

Luke: What's the point of repeating that long list. It sounds *intolerably flat.* My publisher in Antioch would never approve, I think I'll leave out the repetition.

Paul: But if you do, and put 'wife' in the first part, don't you think some people may suppose that a gospel preacher who leaves his wife behind may expect to pick up several more along the way?

Luke: (blushing) Well . . . I suppose that's possible.

Paul: And I like that touch of 'mothers' in the plural. That's not 'flat' at all. I can think of so many Christian women who welcome me into their homes and treat me like a son of the house.

Luke: True. But I can't stand repeating that long list. I'm afraid 'mothers' will have to go . . . sorry! And I'll certainly keep 'wife' in the first part. Wait till Priscilla reads *my gospel!*

What do these skits show?

1. The absurdity of a man like Aquila wishing to change the words of Christ as reported by Peter.

2. The absurdity of Dr. Luke being swayed by such petty motives as literary finesse and personal jealousy. (Of course it is also absurd to find him reading Mark's Gospel with Paul in Caesarea; but according to the critics he must have 'copied' it *somewhere*).

The only theory that accounts for the differences *and* the correspondences is the old one: that Matthew, Peter, and Luke's informant all heard Jesus hold a longer conversation on this subject, and each made his own precis according to the words which specially impressed him. That the three passages in the three Gospels were written independently is confirmed by the fact that

a. Each has a different way of expressing 'everyone'.

Matthew — 'everyone who has left shall receive . . .'
Mark — 'there is no one who . . . *unless* he receives . . .'
Luke — 'there is no one . . . who shall *not* receive . . .'

b. The three passages complement each other:

1. If we had only Matthew, we might think that the reward was heavenly, whereas in Mark it is apparent that the reward will be given on *earth*.

2. The fact that 'wife' comes only once (in Luke) whereas 'brothers' etc. are mentioned in all three, shows, I suggest, that the call of God often entails a man leaving his *parents'* home, but much less often his *own* home. This agrees with the Bible's general teaching on the supreme importance of the marriage vow.

Conclusion

Our theological critics' attempt to probe Luke's mind is as unsuccessful as the literary critics' attempt to diagnose

Thomas Hughes. We suggest that the only theory that makes sense of the whole Gospel panorama is the old theory of inspiration and guidance by the Holy Spirit. Each writer, having heard Christ's words himself or from an eye/ear-witness, recorded his own independent summary of what was said. When we put all three summaries together we find an interlocking mosaic of truth. Our Evangelists combine to make a beautiful harmony of teaching — because the score has been written by one great Composer.

CHAPTER SIXTEEN

Why Curse a Tree?

'The static, the over-simplified will have to go; we shall be forced to make the bridge between "gentle Jesus" and the "wrath of the Lamb".'

Dorothy Sayers

On Mark 11:12—14 and 20—25 Professor Nineham writes: 'This story is one of the most difficult in the Gospels for it approximates more closely than any other to the type of 'unreasonable' miracle characteristic of the non-canonical Gospel literature.'

It will be helpful to take a look at one of these apocryphal stories to which he refers:

'Again he went through the village, and a child ran and dashed against his shoulder. And Jesus was provoked and said unto him, Thou shalt not finish thy course. And immediately he fell down and died . . .' (Apocryphal NT p.50)

Nineham continues: '. . . the fundamental objection to the historicity of the (fig tree) story . . . is that the action ascribed to Jesus seems completely out of character.' He then quotes with approval another commentator who says: 'It is irrational and revolting . . . and lacks any sort of justification.' Later, in his note on v. 13 ('he found nothing but leaves, for it was not the season for figs') we find this comment:

'The words have never satisfactorily been explained.'

Now we may readily admit that the story is not without difficulty. The average schoolboy who lights upon it for the first time might say, 'Well, that's rum. Rather like what my

Dad does when breakfast isn't ready — bangs the table and shouts at Mum!' But scholars are expected to show more patience and understanding than schoolboys.

Since the days of Irenaeus it has often been pointed out that there is an analogy between the works of God in Nature and the words of God in Scripture. Psalm 19 says the same. In both Nature and Scripture there are difficulties. But the scientist faced with an apparent anomaly (e.g. the expansion of water when freezing) does not throw up his hands and shout, 'This is out of character — it can't be true!'. Rather, he sits down quietly, investigates thoroughly, thinks hard, and finally comes up with another 'law' which can explain *both* the expansion of water *and* the contraction of other liquids. His fundamental conviction is that all nature must be harmonious; and so, in the end, it proves to be.

Thus it has always been with true Christian scholars. One of the finest of these in the 19th Century was Richard Chenevix Trench, Archbishop of Dublin. For his immense learning he finds a place in the Encyclopaedia Britannica, which informs us that he 'gave the first impulse to the great Oxford New English Dictionary'; but to the Christian public he is best known for his *Notes on the Parables* (1841) and *Notes on the Miracles* (1846), 'popular works which are treasures of erudite and acute illustration'. (Both these books ran through many editions and it is an enormous pity that they have been allowed to go out of print in Britain).[1]

Trench patiently investigated comments on the fig tree incident from early Christian times, did some hard thinking and comparison of Scripture with Scripture, and reached the conclusion that every apparent difficulty can be explained. Here is a brief summary of his arguments:

A. The Moral problem:

   1. Jesus did thousands of miracles of mercy but only one of judgment.
   2. The tree belonged to nobody so nobody suffered loss.
   3. The tree was inanimate so could not suffer pain.

1. But they can still be obtained from Baker Book House, Grand Rapids, Michigan.

4. The purpose was not to terrify opponents but to edify disciples.

B. The Botanical problem:

1. On some kinds of fig tree, fruit appears before the leaves. (the Roman naturalist Pliny remarks on this odd fact).

2. Therefore, even though it was not the proper season for figs (so other fig trees had *neither* fruit *nor* leaves), a tree which had leaves might reasonably be expected to have fruit too.

3. Christ was disappointed not because it had no fruit, but because having leaves it *yet* had no fruit. In this respect the tree presented an exact parallel to the Jewish nation, which boasted the outward and visible forms of religion but lacked the inward and spiritual fruit of righteousness.

It seems strange that our commentator could have read all this and yet still be capable of writing, 'It has never been satisfactorily explained'.

CHAPTER SEVENTEEN

Did Jesus interpret Parables?

'There is no reason to suppose that each story was told on one occasion only. On the contrary, it seems most likely that they were repeated over and over again — sometimes in identical words, sometimes with variations.

Dorothy Sayers

It is an axiom of modern scholarship that Jesus himself did not interpret his parables, so all interpretations were made up by 'the Church' and tacked onto the story — sometimes missing the point altogether. (This is a neat way of avoiding a head-on clash with the Master. It would be rash for a scholar to pretend to greater wisdom than the Son of God's, but his underlings may well have erred.) So we are taught to attribute all 'hard sayings' to the apostles, and persuade ourselves that we now understand where they went wrong. Thus it is with the parables of the Sower, the Tares, and the Drag-Net: Matthew is blamed for *forcing* an unnatural explanation upon Jesus' words (AWA p. 103: '. . . the forced nature of the interpretation is shown by the fact that what is sown is made to indicate the kind of hearer, whereas it *should* represent the Gospel.' O fortunate us to have been born in an age which has at last perceived what all the saints and scholars of nineteen centuries mistook!)

Perhaps the most startling claim of our commentator is found at the end of the parable of the Labourers in the Vineyard (p. 151). *'In the intention of Jesus* (our italics) the parable simply illustrated the teaching that the gift of eternal life is not the reward of human merit but the free gift of divine grace.' Now one recognises that in a school textbook there is not always room for discussion of various interpreta-

tions, but surely this comment is somewhat over-dogmatic?
And any schoolboy can see that it does not make sense, because the labourers *did* work for their penny, so it was *not* a
free gift! What a pity that A. W. Argyle did not (apparently)
consult his predecessor in the C.U.P. series, Rev. A. Carr, who
gives about 400 well-chosen words to the explanation, pointing out that the parable was directed to Peter's question
('what shall we have?') and relates to Christian *service,* not to
salvation. 'The disciples . . . must beware of a spirit very
prevalent among hard workers, and not think too much of
their own labours . . .'

Similarly we find Prof. D. E. Nineham claiming that 'most
commentators regard' Mark 12:10—11 ('the stone which the
builders rejected . . .') 'as an addition made when the parable
of the Wicked Husbandmen was already interpreted allegori-
cally'. What Nineham means, I think, is most *modern* commentators that *he has read.* Back in 1865 Bishop J. C. Ryle found
it necessary to consult 79 commentaries in order to write his
Expository Thoughts on the Gospels, and many more have
been written since then — in scores of languages. So Nineham's
claim may be somewhat over-optimistic. He is again thinking
in terms of the village pond and forgetting the world-wide
ocean. The vast majority of commentators, in fact, do not even
mention the possibility of Mark 12:10—11 being an addition,
because it makes excellent sense and no manuscript has ever
been seen that omits these verses. The 'addition' idea is
simply a figment of the imagination of modern scholars
obsessed with their own hypotheses.

Interpretation of the Parable of the Sower

But the argument (against 'the Church' making up interpretations) is much stronger yet. Modern scholars have not begun
to answer such practical questions as, Where was the 'alle-
gorization' of the parable of the Sower first written? At Rome?
Jerusalem? Antioch? And if Matthew and Luke copied Mark's
'addition', why did they do it so badly? Why did they introduce so many changes in *language* which add up to no-change-
at-all in *meaning*? It is hard enough to believe that *one*
interpretation not spoken by Christ could have crept into *one*

Gospel; but to suggest that 3 independent pseudo-interpretations could have crept into 3 different Gospels published in 3 different places at 3 different times, is to stretch our credulity beyond breaking point.

In order to show just how independent these three interpretations are, we shall illustrate the *verbal* problem as a *numerical* problem, thus:

Matthew *(28 verbs)*	Mark *(27 verbs)*	Luke *(23 verbs)*
5 (comes)	5 (comes)	5 (comes)
11	36	53
6 (becomes)	6 (becomes)	54
12	37	55
13	38	57
14	3 (are)	3 (are)
15	39	58
16	2 (takes up)	2 (takes up)
17	8 (they hear)	8 (they hear)
18	40	59
19	7 (they have)	7 (they have)
	41	60
20	42	61
21	1 (they are)	1 (they are)
22	43	62
23	9 (having heard)	9 (having heard
24	44	63
25	10 (they are)	10 (they are)
4 (having come)	4 (having come)	56
26	45	64
27	46	65
28	47	66
29	48	
30	49	122
67	100	
68	101	
69	149	
70		
301		
——	——	——
1000	1000	1000

Explanation

1. Each number represents one Greek verb.
2. The numbers in each column adding up to 1000 represent the fact that the total *meaning* of the interpretation in each Gospel is exactly the same; but the numbers all being different (except for ten of them) show that each writer uses different verbs or a different part of the same verb.
3. Note that out of 78 verbs used, only one ('he comes') is common to all three writers.
4. Matthew shares with Mark only 3 out of their combined total of 55 verbs.
5. Mark shares with Luke only 8 out of their combined total of 50 verbs. How can this be accounted for if any one writer copied from any other?
6. This by no means represents all the differences. For instance, each writer uses a different word for the Devil:

> Matthew — 'the evil one'
> Mark — 'Satan'
> Luke — 'the devil'

Why should any copier change any one of these to any other, since all three are synonyms?

Conclusion

The hypothesis of Professors Dodd and Nineham that the interpretation is an 'early Christian creation' breaks down completely under close examination. Devoid of all historical or linguistic support, it is an unsuccessful attempt to drive a wedge between the brilliant Master and his 'dull-witted' disciples. On the other hand our three records have just the kind of similarities and dissimilarities one would expect if three ear-witnesses condensed and reported *independently* the very words of Christ.

Why only three parables interpreted?

Positively, can we see any reason that might have led Jesus to interpret *some* of the parables and leave the rest unexplained?
The following is offered as a suggestion.

Teachers of arithmetic normally
  a. work out a few examples on the board
  b. check to make sure all pupils understand the basic principles
  c. set a row of sums for pupils to work out for themselves.

This corresponds quite closely with the procedure followed by Christ:
  a. He interpreted in detail the parables of the Sower, the Tares and the Drag-Net.
  b. He asked the disciples whether they had understood (Matthew 13:51)
  c. From this point on He did not usually explain the parables. (But Luke 15:7 and 10 are really mini-interpretations).

Finally, the critics' theory (that Jesus did not interpret) runs contrary to common sense and logic. For if the apostles (or 'early Church') thought it necessary to interpret *three* parables, why did they not do the same for the remaining 27? Are these so simple that they require no interpretation or so difficult that they defy it? If the work had been done by a Religious Education Board, we can be sure they would have put out an Authorised Interpretation for every parable, neatly rounded off with no loose ends. (And of course they would never have left the four Gospels as they are, full of *apparent* discrepancies. Everything would have been smoothed out, to silence objectors). The very *un*tidiness of the Gospels is another indication of their divine inspiration, because Nature too is untidy. We may be sure that Christ either deliberately left 27 parables uninterpreted — because He knew the Holy Spirit would later show their meaning to the apostles and the Church; or though He did interpret them to the apostles (Mark 4:34), divine wisdom did not see fit to include the interpretation in the written record. As we have seen (chapter 2), brevity was essential if the whole world was to have the Gospel, and usually the translator/teacher goes with the printed word to explain it.

'I find in the Bible', says Cecil, 'a grand peculiarity, that seems to say to all who attempt to systematize it, I am not of your kind . . . I stand alone. The great and the wise shall never exhaust my treasures: by figures and parables I will come down to the feelings and understandings of the ignorant.' ('The Bible Handbook', Joseph Angus).

CHAPTER EIGHTEEN

Modern Scholars' False Analogies

1 — Picture Restoration

'. . . *each " historical Jesus" is unhistorical. The documents say what they say and cannot be added to; each new "historical Jesus" therefore has to be got out of them by suppression at one point and exaggeration at another, and by that sort of guessing* (brilliant *is the adjective we teach humans to apply to it*) *on which no one would risk ten shillings in ordinary life.'*

C. S. Lewis, 'The Screwtape Letters'

Modern scholars use a number of analogies and illustrations by which they try to persuade us that their picture of Jesus is true and the traditional Gospel picture is false. Let us first examine the 'picture-restoration' analogy as presented by Dr. J. A. T. Robinson:

'. . . it is possible — I would think probable — that Jesus' words have been interpreted to fit such ways of thinking in the early Church. In this case *our Bibles do not contain what Jesus said or meant* . . . the only way is to go to the evidence . . . as the picture restorer would go to the layers of superimposed paint, and patiently reconstruct what is likely to be most original.' (CWTNT p. 19)

A good example of picture-restoration is provided by the *Daily Telegraph* of 31 January 1979 under the headline:

DECEIT OF PORDENONE'S 'LADY' UNCOVERED.

We quote from Terence Mullaly's article:

'Sometime in the 19th Century the woman's face was extensively re-painted, which gave her a wide-eyed, somewhat sentimental and sweet appearance. At the same time her hair was painted brown.

During restoration the original face was found to be in good condition underneath the re-paint. The lady is now seen to be a blonde and her expression has been completely transformed.'

Now let us see whether Robinson's analogy really fits. The first point to note is that under the re-paint there was *real solid old paint.* But when you call some verses 'additions' and chip them away from the Gospels, you find underneath *nothing at all.* There is no palette from which to fill the gap but the palette of your own imagination. If we were studying the life of Socrates we might well chip off a piece of Plato and replace it with a piece of Xenophon or Aeshines, because they are reliable contemporary writers who had met and talked with him; but every scholar knows that for the life and message of Christ we have *no* contemporary records other than our four Gospels. So imagination sets to work, and before long we have a Jesus fashioned by the verbal craftsman hardly less fictional than the painted clay gods of Hindu mythology. One scholar does not like the Virgin Birth, so he cuts out the first two chapters of Luke (the 'great scholar' Julius Wellhausen did just that in his edition of the Gospel). Another scholar dislikes teaching about Hell, so he claims that Mark 9:48 'affords no ground for attributing to Jesus the later fully developed doctrines of eternal punishment' (DN p. 258). A third thinks the children shouting praises in the Temple 'is probably Matthew's *invention*' (AWA p. 158). The point to remember is that it is all a matter of taste and distaste and nothing to do with scholarship or learning.

A better analogy for all this, we think, could be drawn from sculpture. An apprentice finds a heroic figure hewn from marble and tries to improve it. He sets to work chipping here and polishing there, changing the expression and the posture. But all he does is to *de*tract from the original, spoiling the perfect balance and symmetry of the masterpiece. No latent beauties are discovered; no unsuspected harmonies revealed. The resultant form is uncouth, misshapen, incomplete. So it is with modern scholars and the Gospels. Each fashions his own Jesus in his own image, and the character that emerges, stunted and blunted, is a sorry approximation to the real Christ of history.

The second point to note is that Mr. Mullaly calls this repainting 'deceit'. I believe he is right. I believe 99 people out of 100 would agree. Re-painting is deceiving; so also is re-writing speeches so that the speaker is made to say *not* what he said but what you want them to *think* he said. So once again we come up against the moral problem which is, I believe, an impassable stumbling-block to the chopping/ changing/copying theory. The apostles themselves must have been cheats and liars either to write the Gospels or to allow them to circulate knowing, as they must have known (supposing the theory to be true), that they did '*not* contain what Jesus said or meant.' To this 'reductio ad absurdum' I see no answer.

Speeches in secular historians

However, it is sometimes urged, in extenuation of the apostles' alleged falsehoods, that secular historians in the ancient world often made up speeches to fit the occasion, so nobody would have blamed the Evangelists for doing the same. It would almost have been expected of them to follow the time-honoured convention. 'Everyone knows that Plato's Socrates is at least half Plato himself' — so the argument runs — 'so it would be quite understandable if Matthew/Mark/Luke/John mixed in their own ideas with the Sayings of Jesus.' (see also p. 128).

In order to get this 'parallel' into better focus it will be helpful to study a paragraph from the Greek historian Thucydides (460—400 B.C.). 'In this history I have made use of set speeches . . . I have found it difficult to remember the precise words used in the speeches which I listened to myself and my various informants have experienced the same difficulty; so my method has been, while keeping as closely as possible to the general sense of the words that were actually used, to make the speakers say what, in my opinion, was called for by each situation.'

Now, is this the way our Evangelists wrote up Jesus' speeches? Let us note some of the differences:

1. 'Difficult to remember'. We have dealt with this problem

in Appendix II (p. 101). The apostles had the help of the Holy Spirit, whereas Thucydides was on his own. Also, they had a corporate memory of 12, very much better than one. Thirdly, much of Christ's teaching, being of universal application, must have been repeated many times; whereas most of Thucydides' speeches were of temporary and topical interest only.

2. 'My various informants'. Educationists inform us that we remember only one tenth of what we hear, so the casual listener in a crowd is not a reliable reporter. But the attention accorded by the 120 (Acts 1) to their long-awaited Messiah is likely to have been considerably greater than the Athenians' to Cleon or even Pericles.

3. 'What was called for by each situation'. Here, to my mind, we have the sharpest dividing line between secular history and Gospel history. For 'never man spake like this Man!' (John 7:46). On almost every occasion Jesus' words were *un*called for, and unexpected. Familiarity with the text has bred in all of us a degree of contempt which is notice-ably lacking in new readers. ('Pah! He had *power*!' exclaimed one who had just read Mark newly-translated into an African language). But even in London in 1978 Alex McCowen was able to fill a theatre night after night simply by reciting the 'simplest' Gospel from memory. It is full of surprises, with never a dull moment; and for unpredictable repartee, only Dr. Johnson comes anywhere near Jesus.

Consider one example: His reply to the question 'Why do you teach in parables?' Anyone who doesn't know would ex-pect Him to say, 'Because it makes spiritual truths easier to understand'. But Jesus says just the opposite: '. . . that hearing they may hear and *not* understand!' Other unforget-table sayings come to mind:

'Solomon in all his glory was not arrayed as one of these'
'Why do you call me good?'
'Whose image and superscription is this?'
'Do quickly what you are going to do . . .' (to Judas Iscariot)
'Go tell that fox . . .'
'Who touched me?'
      . . . the list is endless.

And such *uncalled for* remarks, it is safe to say, could never have been invented by rabbis, philosophers, or even Galilean fishermen. Further confirmation is provided by the fact that no publisher has ever made a long-term success of selling a modern scholar's 'restoration' of any one Gospel.

Moffat's translation

Today few people under 30 have seen Moffat's translation of the Bible but in the 1920's it enjoyed quite a vogue. James Moffat, D.D., D.Litt., was a very learned man, but his Bible was a printer's nightmare. The O.T. presented a strange aspect with alternating kinds of type — for Moffat's foible was transposition. Chunks of text were wrenched from their traditional setting and thrust into others supposed to be more suitable — usually without any MS authority. John's Gospel alone suffered 10 of these, including the insertion of chapters 15 and 16 between 13:31 (a) and 13:31 (b).

The Moffat Bible soon went out of fashion. Today you would be lucky to find one in a Christian bookshop. Why? Because the editor was too clever: too much regard for his own opinions and too little respect for historical evidence. Critical scholars have learned the lesson and (I suspect) dare not experiment again with a mangled text. They know it would not sell. But they continue to mangle it with sharp comments. Consider for example this from A. E. Harvey's *Companion to the Gospels:*

'When John came to write this part (chapters 13–17) of his gospel, he was doubtless influenced by the historian's *convention* of writing a long parting speech *purporting* to have been made by the hero shortly before his death . . . John's is not the only Gospel to make use of this *convention:* in Luke's Gospel, Jesus' last supper is also *made the occasion* for a parting speech . . .'

Note the pejorative use of the word 'convention', which, with 'purporting', clearly implies that Jesus did not actually say what He is reported to have said at that time. This is rather like saying:

'It was a *convention* for a commander to signal the fleet an Order of the Day before a great battle. This *convention* doubtless influenced the naval historian when he *made Trafalgar the occasion* for Nelson's famous "England expects that every man will do his duty", *purporting* to be the hero's signal shortly before his death.'

Common sense rejects such a 'reconstruction'; common sense which owes nothing to scholarship but judges of probability as to how men speak and act in real life. And if Dr. Johnson was right in his opinion that 'by the common sense of readers uncorrupted with literary prejudice . . . must be finally decided all claim to poetical honours', so also it is true, we think, that by the common sense of Christians uncorrupted with theological prejudices must be finally decided all claim to historical truth in sacred literature. All we know of Nelson leads us to believe that it was indeed he who originated that particular signal at that particular time; and all we know of the Lord Jesus Christ assures us that He did indeed speak the words recorded in John 13—17 on the night of His betrayal.

So once again we find ourselves in agreement with C. S. Lewis: the historical Jesus is the traditional Jesus, and the Christ of the critics is a fake.

CHAPTER NINETEEN

Modern Scholars' False Analogies

2 — Cathedral Guide

'It has been said that though God cannot alter the past, historians can.'

Samuel Butler

Professor Nineham likens his commentary to a guide showing visitors round an ancient building. This would be a felicitous illustration were it not for one flaw. His assumption throughout the actual text is that those farthest away in time from the date of building are better able to judge the purpose of the architect and describe the process of construction, than those who were friends of the architect and saw it taking shape. As a guide to St. Paul's, Nineham would, on this analogy, prefer a modern handbook to Samuel Pepys or Isaac Newton (supposing they had left us a description). He goes so far as to say that 'if the Gospels are read without any knowledge of their origins and consequent character, positive misunderstanding is likely to be the result'. But where is a 'knowledge of their origins' likely to be found? In the literature of the ancient Church or in the literature of modern Europe?

Pursuing his 'farthest away, clearest view' idea, Nineham substitutes guesswork for history. Whereas in St. Paul's we find marble slabs commemorating *real* people who were born, lived and died, on definite dates, most of Nineham's characters are shadowy anonymities. We know not whence they came nor whither they went. Open the book almost anywhere and you will read something like this.

'The teaching of v. 27 does not lead on very naturally to

that of v.28ff, which *appears* to connect rather with v.21. *Probably* vv.29–30 reached Mark as an unattached saying . . . He therefore attached it to vv.17–27 by means of the saying *attributed* to Peter in v.28, though *originally* it seems to have envisaged a wider circle than the twelve. There is considerable *uncertainty* about the *original* wording and meaning of v.30 . . . In any case according to a large number of commentators, the words after "hundredfold" are an interpetative *addition* to the saying, made by the early Christians and *reflecting* their experience . . .' (our italics).

One may well ask, who were these early Christians? When did they first 'reflect' on their experiences and put them into writing? How did they manage to persuade other Christians that Christ had spoken words which (according to 'large numbers of commentators') He never spoke? Who attributed Peter a saying which he did not say? How do we know what it was originally? Who was Mark? (quite uncertain, according to Nineham). To none of these questions does Nineham give an answer that can be called historical. All is speculation, unalloyed by any vein of solid evidence. You might as well attempt to find the name and address of every man who helped to build the Cathedral and say which stones he laid, as sort out the inextricable confusion of Nineham's hunt for 'originals'. But real books by real authors do not get strung together in this way. It would be difficult, I think, to find any modern parallel for such (alleged) patchwork cobbling; and I do not recall any in the classical literature of Greece and Rome — at least after 500 B.C.

St. Paul's Cathedral was not built by a committee of bumbling amateurs. It bears the unmistakable stamp of a master mind. So does each of the Gospels. Nor can we press the analogy to infer that because St. Paul's took 36 years to build, so each (or any) Gospel took a generation to put together. A good typist could finish Mark's Gospel in a morning, and a skilled Greek amanuensis could take down the original inside a day. Allowing time for correction, revision etc. there is no reason to think that any Gospel took more than a week to write. The *preparation had been going on for years* in the mind of Matthew etc. as they taught and preached.

When they finally put pen to paper, the words probably came pretty fast.

When we turn to Nineham's index, under the heading *Early Christian Writings* we find 38 references, whereas modern (1850—1960) writers are quoted *614 times.* Contrast this with J. B. Lightfoot's 328 early Christian passages (in Essays on *Supernatural Religion*) and only 215 modern authors. Lightfoot believed that recorded *history* was the key to the origins of our Gospels. Nineham dismisses history as 'tradition' and (with very few exceptions) confines his research to a small coterie of like-minded scholars.

One quotation of an early Christian writer in Nineham is particularly interesting. When discussing the Last Twelve Verses of Mark he refers to Eusebius as 'the great scholar' because *on this one point* Eusebius' opinion coincides with his own. But Nineham quotes Eusebius only twice (J. B. Lightfoot quotes him 89 times) and omits to tell us that this 'great scholar' who had access to hundreds of documents now lost, and had talked to Christians from all over the Roman Empire — this learned Bishop informs us that the first Gospel was written by Matthew the apostle, the second by Mark the companion of Peter, the third by Luke the companion of Paul, and the fourth by the apostle John. Not only does he tell us this in his own words but he also quotes the testimonies of Papias, bishop of Hierapolis, of Irenaeus, bishop of Lyons, of Clement and Origen of Alexandria. Nothing could be more certain, in the view of this famous Church historian, than that our Gospels are authentic, apostolic, and divinely inspired. (See also p. 158)

All this mass of evidence Nineham brushes aside in a footnote (p. 39): '. . . for it is not clear that these writers had any source of information other than the Papias tradition.' (A great many things are 'not clear' about the years 70—150 A.D. because only a few fragments of literature have survived. Lightfoot calls it the Dark Age of the Church.) Nineham seems not to realise that well-known facts do not become well known because they are written down in books: *they are written down in books because they are well known.* 'Never in the field of human conflict was so much owed by so many to so few' is a sentence that has passed into the currency of our language, so that it is quoted and parodied by Englishmen the world over. A historian writing in 3900 A.D. might suggest: 'It is not clear that these writers had any source of information other than the Oxford Dictionary of Quotations' — but he would be completely wrong. *The quotation was put in the book because it was already in the minds and mouths of millions of Englishmen.*

So with the authorship of the Gospels: they were credited to Matthew, Mark, Luke and John *not* because Papias (or Justin or Tertullian or Irenaeus or Origen) chose to stick these labels on them, but because the *fact* of their authorship had been talked about, thought about, taught and preached and written about — and never disputed — until by 150 A.D. it was well known to all the hundreds of churches throughout the Roman Empire.

These seem to me good reasons for rejecting the 'farthest-away-clearest view' hypothesis, and for accepting as our guide to the Gospels those who lived 18 centuries nearer to the authors than we do.

CHAPTER TWENTY

Modern Scholars' False Analogies

3 — *Genesis and the Gospels*

'The science of theology is nothing else but grammar exercised on the words of the Holy Spirit'.

Martin Luther

This is (to me) the most interesting and important of our 'false analogies'. Indeed it is not false at all: but it leads to a conclusion exactly the opposite of that which the author intended. Important, because it also suggests that the way back to belief in the truth of Christianity in the 1980's is not through literary criticism, not through archaeology, but through scientific *reconstruction of pre-history*.

Dr. J. A. T. Robinson (CWTNT) devotes two pages to drawing a parallel between (a) the early chapters of Genesis and (b) the early chapters of Matthew and Luke. He believes that both (a) and (b) are full of 'myth'. Bishop Wilberforce (1860), he opines, grievously erred 'in insisting that the opening chapters of Genesis were literally and historically true'. 'The truth of the Gospel stories involves indeed a more complex inter-relationship of fact and interpretation — for Jesus, unlike Adam, *was* a historical individual.'

This appears to mean that, since the story of Adam is *pure* fiction, it does not require much wit to allegorise or spiritualise the whole thing; but the story of Jesus is a *mixture* of fact and fiction, so you have to be really smart (or a modern scholar) to see which is which, sift the wheat from the chaff, etc.

Turning on to chapter 6 (CWTNT) we find: 'The centre of interest of Matthew 1 is not gynaecology, *any more than* that

of Genesis is geology. Once we forget this and start asking
prosaic or scientific 'How?' questions rather than meaningful
or interpretative 'Why?' questions (whether of the opening
chapters of the Old Testament or the New), then not only do
we miss the point for ourselves: we put stumbling blocks in
the way of other people. Doubtless there is some history
behind the story of the Flood . . . so too the marvellous
stories of the annunciation and the virgin birth, the wise men
and the shepherds . . . may indeed reflect fact. But to take
it all, with the fundamentalists, *as prose rather than poetry*[1]
is to confound everything . . .' (pp. 96/7)

First, I am delighted to find myself in complete agreement
with Robinson as to the unity of Scripture. He believes, as I
do, that each type of literature — history, poetry or prophecy
— should be interpreted according to its own *genre*. And if
Genesis 1—11 be poetry, I am fully prepared to admit that
Matthew 1 and 2 and Luke 1 and 2 may be poetry too. The
logic of this argument is incontestable.

For Genesis bears on its face all the marks of plain prose
narrative (as I have argued at length elsewhere[2]), divided into
eleven sections by the key phrase 'these are the generations
. . .' *If* such a book can be twisted by interpretation so that
'one day' = 1,000,000,000 years, so that 'after its kind' =
after many kinds; so that 'the Lord God formed man of the
dust of the ground' means that man evolved from an ape, and
'the rib which the Lord God had taken from the man, He
built into a woman' means that the female of the species
evolved from an ape-woman; *then* we cannot deny that
'interpretation' may also be allowed to twist the Nativity
stories, and everything else in the Gospels, to fit the measure
of man's mind. But if Dr. Robinson's premise is false; if
Genesis *is* concerned with geology, especially Flood geology;
if Darwin's theory remains an hypothesis unproven and
unprovable, demanding 'faith in the fossils which have never
been found, faith in the embryological evidence which does
not exist, faith in the experiments which refuse to come off'
— then of course Robinson's argument against the Gospel
collapses and his conclusion is entirely wrong.

1. See next chapter.
2. *The Great Brain Robbery*, chapter 2.

It is remarkable that Dr. Robinson seems quite unaware of Morris and Whitcomb's epoch-making *The Genesis Flood* published in 1961. Now in its 20th edition, this devastating attack on Darwinism and Lyellism ('the-earth-is-millions-of-years-old') has persuaded a large number of professional scientists and educators that the Bible may, after all, give the true account of origins and 'pre-history'. Already ten States of the USA have passed laws enacting that 'creationism' should be taught parallel with the theory of evolution in secondary schools. 'Creation literature' now runs to a score of major volumes and hundreds of learned articles. These demonstrate from many different angles that the brute facts of Nature agree far better with the doctrine of creation than with evolution. God actually meant what He said in Genesis, as our forefathers believed: He really created species distinct, and He really sent a global Flood.

So Dr. Robinson's link between Genesis and the Gospels, which forty years ago would have furnished a plausible argument for myth and legend in *both,* turns out to be very strong evidence on the other side. Where it is possible to test Bible statements by scientific research (e.g. the impossibility of cross-breeding between species, and the gigantic fossil graveyards) we find them precisely true. We therefore have good grounds for believing that where it is *not* possible to test Bible statements (e.g. in the Gospels), they are nevertheless equally true. The literal interpretation is the correct interpretation, and we have no excuse for thinking otherwise: We can appeal to no precedent of myth, legend or folk-lore in the Old Testament, because none has been proved to exist.

In the early days of the Church, men believed Genesis because they knew the Gospels were true. Today, 65 generations removed from Christ's apostles, the *stones* cry out that Genesis is true, *therefore* believe the Gospels. As at the Renaissance 'Greece arose from the dead with the New Testament in her hand', so in these last days Prehistory has arisen from the dead with the book of Genesis in her hand, and the message is the Lord's.

'If you believed Moses, you would believe me, for he wrote of me. But if you believe not his writings, how shall you believe My words?' (John 5:47)

CHAPTER TWENTY-ONE

The Infancy Narratives

'The rejection as unhistorical of all passages which narrate miracles is sensible if we start by knowing that the miraculous in general never occurs.'

C. S. Lewis, 'Fern-seed and Elephants'

Genesis 1 can not be called poetry, because it has neither the parallelism nor the repetition characteristic of Hebrew poetry. The case for poetry in the Infancy Narratives is, if possible, weaker still. For ancient Greek poetry had rigid rules of scansion. Even in the 1st century A.D., long after the classical period, Greeks were still composing in the old classical hexameter and elegiac couplets. But Matthew and Luke show no trace of this rhythm; in fact Luke's frequent use of the Hebriac 'it came to pass' makes the narrative about as prosaic as it can be.

This is not to say there is no poetry in Luke 1—2. From early days the Magnificat and Benedictus have been recognised as (Hebrew-style) poetry; but they are (in effect) hymns, not narrative. Here we have *typical Hebrew parallelism*:

He hath showed strength
   He hath scattered the proud
He hath put down princes
   and hath exalted them of low degree
He hath filled the hungry
   and the rich He hath sent empty away
and

typical figures of speech:

horn of salvation
dayspring from on high
those that sit in darkness and the shadow of death

Thus it is evident that Luke, knowing well what poetry was, deliberately avoided it when telling the story of Christ's birth. There is only *one* figure of speech in the Infancy narratives: 'And thou, Bethlehem . . .' — and that is Micah's, not Matthew's. Everything else is told in plain prose, unadorned and unambiguous.

Folk-tales — Fairy tales?

Why then does Dr. Robinson declaim so confidently about 'stories with all the legendary and mythical beauty of folk-tales'? I believe part of the answer may lie in childhood memories of December 25th, with *poetic* carols ('While shepherds watched . . .' etc.) and the *legend* of Father Christmas. 'When I became a man, I put away childish things.' It is easy to forget that the original author of the shepherd-story is reckoned by modern historians to be unsurpassed as an accurate reporter of Roman provincial affairs in the 1st century. And it is *this* man who records angelic visitations and the Virgin Birth, carefully noting names, times and places. If this is not history, we submit, then nothing written in the 1st century has any claim to be called history. And it seems unreasonable to admit the possibility of miraculous events in the last chapter while denying the possibility in the first. True Christianity is miraculous from start to finish; but half-baked Christianity is a myth and a delusion, the folk-lore invention of 20th century theological colleges.

Maternal memories

A difficulty encountered by many biographers is — how to portray the hero's childhood when his mother is dead? Writers who rushed into print at the end of World War II found it hard to reconstruct Hitler's early life at Linz, because his mother had died in 1907. In the ancient world it was much the same. Julius Caesar's mother died two years before the assassination, which perhaps partly accounts for the fact that neither Suetonius nor Plutarch say anything about his first 15 years. Even at the end of the 1st century A.D. there was uncertainty about the birth-year of Emperor Tiberius (died 37 A.D.). Also, superstition clung to the birth-places of V.I.P.'s. Seutonius relates how a man sleeping in the room where Augustus had been born (a century earlier) 'was hurled out of bed by a supernatural agency and found lying half-dead against the door, bed-clothes and all!'. Tales such as this may account for scholars' scepticism when we come to the childhood stories of Jesus. But we should bear in mind two important differences:

1. Mary was at the Cross (John 19:26) and with the disciples in Jerusalem (Acts 1:14). Supposing her to have been about 17 when Jesus was born, there is no reason why she should not have met Luke when he came to Jerusalem (Acts 21:17). She would then have been aged 80 or 81, and many women over 80 have extremely clear minds and memories. The strong Hebraic tinge of Luke's first two chapters is just what we would expect if she was his informant, as 2:19 suggests.

2. Alone among all those who have walked this planet, Jesus knew from the beginning the exact year and day of His death — and of Joseph, Mary's husband. Supposing Joseph to have been alive during the early part of Christ's ministry — as seems almost required by John 6:42 — it would have been very easy for Matthew (perhaps at Jesus' suggestion) to interview him about his dreams and the Virgin Birth.

So both Matthew and Luke had an enormous advantage over biographers of other men: opportunities of hearing from the 'parents' themselves exactly how God stage-managed the entry of His Son, heralded to believers by stars and angels but hidden from malice and murder by direct divine intervention. To those still tempted to doubt the veracity of the Infancy Narratives I would recommend reading (a) the myths that surrounded the birth of Alexander the Great (according to Plutarch) and (b) the Infancy Gospels in the Apocryphal N.T. By contrast with pagan fantasies and 'pious' fiction, our Gospels carry the unmistakable ring of truth.

CHAPTER TWENTY-TWO

Modern Scholars' False Analogies

4 — Mark 13 and Daniel

> 'Any statement put into our Lord's mouth by the old
> texts, which, if he had really made it, would constitute a
> prediction of the future, is taken to have been put in after
> the occurrence which it seemed to predict. This is very
> sensible if we start by knowing that inspired prediction can
> never occur.'
>
> C. S. Lewis, 'Fern-seed and Elephants'

To enter this chapter with Professor Nineham is to attempt to
hack one's way through a jungle where unsupported
hypotheses grow rank and tall amid dense thickets of
'perhaps', 'maybe', 'presumably', 'it is not certain', 'it has
been suggested', 'quite possibly' etc. etc.

Oh what a tangled web we weave
When first we doubt and won't believe in predictive
prophecy!

With an ingenuity worthy of a better cause, Nineham
labours to prove that Jesus himself spoke few or none of
these words; that the remainder (or all) were culled from
'Daniel' or other Jewish apocalypses, or made up from the
experience of persecuted Christians. And these *bogus* prophecies are supposed to have helped believers to face Nero's
real tortures with a smile. In order to support this strange
hypothesis Nineham finds a precedent in the book of Daniel.
'written *in fact* to bring comfort to the faithful during
terrible times of persecution in the early *second* century B.C.,
it *professes* to reproduce the visions granted to a young Jew

whose life is described as having been lived in Babylon early
in the *sixth* century' (B.C.). (our italics — note the con-
trasts). In other words, Daniel is a forgery; so why should not
Mark 13 be a forgery too?

The question of Daniel's historicity has been referred to an
Appendix; but the probability of such a forgery ever being
written and successfully circulated is directly relevant to our
theme. For who ever heard of a real martyr being sustained
by *fairy-tales*? Is this another case of:

'The toad beneath the harrow knows
Exactly where each tooth-point goes:
The butterfly upon the road
Preaches contentment to that toad' . . .?

But in Nero's persecution there were no 'butterflies' (so far as
we know) in the Christian community: all were toads together.
And there is little point in trying to deceive your own species.
To drop the fable, the only sort of prophecy that would
ever 'comfort the faithful' (B.C. or A.D.) would be genuine
predictions which could have been made *only by divine fore-
sight and inspiration.* The idea that Christian teachers in Rome
would forge prophecies which Christ had never spoken, in
order to encourage the faint-hearted, is a fantasy that breaks
all the laws of moral probability and has no existence, I
daresay, outside the minds of 'modern scholars'.

The Gospel to all nations?

This error is but the beginning of sorrows for our commentator
who compounds it with (a) another psychological blunder and
(b) some very curious editing of the text.

Mark 13:10 reads: 'And the gospel must first be preached
to all the nations.'

a. But we are told that 'verse 10 is commonly regarded as an
insertion into the original document . . . it can hardly be
authentic. For if any such explicit saying had been known,
the early Church would hardly have been as divided as it was
over the question of Gentile converts.' In other words, if
Christ had commanded the apostles to preach to Gentiles, why
all the bother in Acts 10 and 11? Why did Peter need a
special vision to get him moving?

Lord Macaulay has answered these questions, I think, in his essay on Hallam's History. He points out that it was a mistake in the days of Queen Elizabeth I to regard every Roman Catholic as a traitor simply because they owed prime allegiance to the Pope. 'Man is so inconsistent a creature that it is impossible to reason from his belief to his conduct.' Again, every Christian minister would agree in theory that Christ commanded us to preach the gospel everywhere, but missionary societies are not observed to have long queues of volunteers willing to forsake all and evangelise the heathen. (In fact it was 1700 years before European Christians as a whole began to take seriously the Great Commission of Matthew 28:19). So it is nothing remarkable that Jewish believers should have been slow to overcome their pride and prejudice *in spite of* Mark 13:10.

b. In order to get rid of this tiresome verse our commentator now puts forward a theory, not indeed his own, but one which he introduces as a distinct possibility, without criticism. As this is a memorable example of 'modern scholarship' we reproduce it here in full:

'. . . the verse breaks the poetic arrangement apparent in vv. 9 and 11–13 . . . it is, however, possible to punctuate the Greek differently, in which case we get a poetic structure of another sort, and a significantly different meaning:

Take heed to yourselves.
They will deliver you to councils and to synagogues
You will be beaten before (both) governors and kings
You will stand, for my sake, for a testimony to them and
    among the nations.
(Wherever you find yourselves) first preach the gospel;
Then after your arrest by the authorities have no fear,
    etc. . . .'

Comments on the commentary

1. Let me assure non-Grecians that no *Greek* commentator has ever called verses 9, 11, 12, 13 'poetry' or singled out v. 10 as 'breaking the poetical arrangement'. Ancient Greek poetry, like ancient Greek pottery, possessed definite shape and form. It was not just prose chopped into lines, like some modern

English poetry. We do not deny that there is such a thing as rhythmic prose ('. . . we shall fight on the beaches, we shall fight on the landing grounds, we shall fight in the fields and in the streets . . .'), which may include some repetition, but the idea that such prose could not or should not be 'interrupted' by one short staccato sentence, is patently absurd. All the more so when we remember that Matthew, Mark and Luke are probably *condensing* a longer discourse (see chapter 3).

2. The primary meaning of the word *eis* translated 'among' is 'into' or 'towards'. It is translated 'among' only when there is some idea of *motion* in the verb (e.g. Mark 4:18 'they who are sown among thorns'). But here the verb is 'you shall stand' (probably chained or guarded), and it seems very improbable that such a very would be followed by such a preposition. I can find only three places where *eis* is used after 'stand', all in John's Gospel. Twice the phrase is 'into the midst' and once (on the shore'. It is never used of standing among people. So Nineham's translation 'You will stand . . . among the nations' looks improbable.

3. The word 'must' is nearly always used of the fulfilment of Scripture (as above, Mark 13:7). When Jesus wished to give commands, He used the imperative mood ('love your enemies', *not* 'you must love your enemies'). In fact the only example of 'you must' is 'you must be born again', in John 3. In Matthew, Mark and Luke, 'must' is never used with the pronoun 'you'. So the proposed translation 'first preach the gospel' is very misleading. Nineham has substituted the English imperative for the Greek 'must' even when there is no 'you' at all in the Greek.

What Christ meant, almost certainly, was that O.T. prophecy about the gospel being preached to the Gentiles (Isaiah 42 etc.) *must be fulfilled.*

4. 'Then' (last line) is slipped in to lend plausibility to the reconstruction; but again the word is missing in the Greek. There is a perfectly good word for 'then', which Mark uses four times in this chapter (vv. 14, 21, 26, 27), and this would have been another obvious place to use it if he had meant

'*first* preach the gospel . . . *then* do not be anxious . . .'

5. No ancient version lends any support to this extraordinary

punctuation. Jerome's Latin ('et in omnes gentes primum oportet praedicari Evangelium') shows that he took it in exactly the same way as did the translators of our AV, RV, RSV, NEB, GNB and NIV. In fact I would be very surprised to hear of any Bible translator who has ever adopted Professor Nineham's suggestion.

Conclusion

Page 348 of this Pelican Commentary will stand forever as a monument to 'modern scholarship'. Obsessed as our author is with the idea that Jesus could not or would not have predicted the spread of Christianity throughout the world, he tortures[1] the text out of all recognition to prove his point. Defying the laws of grammar, literary usage and scriptural analogy, he punctuates the Word of God as deftly as Quince punctuates his prologue in *A Midsummer Night's Dream*.

1. See 2 Peter 3:16.

CHAPTER TWENTY-THREE

Intimidation of the Ignorant

'. . . *the blindest of all the blind are those who are unable to examine their own presuppositions, and blithely imagine therefore that they do not possess any.*'

Professor Herbert Butterfield,
'Christianity and History' (1949)

Let us refer once again to J. B. Lightfoot's Essays on *Supernatural Religion.*

'There is another more subtle mode of *intimidation* which plays an important part in these volumes. Long lists of references are given in the notes, to modern critics who . . . support the views mentioned or adopted by the author in the text . . . These lists will not fetter the judgment of any thoughtful mind. It is comparatively easy to resist the fallacies of past times, but it is most difficult to escape the infection of the intellectual atmosphere in which we live.'

A century later we find the same weapon — 'literary browbeating', as Lightfoot calls it — playing an important part in our critics' commentaries. Over and over again we are told that 'most commentators' or 'modern scholars' or 'all *competent* scholars' agree on this or that, or reject so-and-so. (And how do we define a competent scholar? Why, a scholar who agrees with *me*, of course!) The writers (JR, DN, AWA, et al.) can get away with these generalisations only because the horizon of most readers is limited to Britain and British books. It would be easy to cite a score of examples to refute the critics' claim to have the big battalions on their side, but I shall pick out just one, from overseas.

Dallas Theological Seminary is committed to the divine inspiration and infallibility of the whole Bible. Every year about 200 students graduate with a Master of Theology degree which requires four years of theological training after university and includes three years of N.T. Greek. And there are 14 more large American theological colleges having (practically) the same doctrinal basis as Dallas. This means that (in the USA alone) between 1970 and 1980 at least ten thousand men will have become Masters of Theology with full faith in Scripture as the Word of God. Add to these — and their predecessors — several hundred faculty members, some of them scholars of international repute. So it would, we think, become British scholars to be rather more cautious in advancing premature claims to a sweeping victory at the polls.

Dangers of dogmatism

As a final warning against this kind of error, we might consider a quotation from the Roman historian Tacitus, a man of undoubted genius (Pliny wrote to him: 'I know your *Histories* will be immortal . . .'). We may pardon him for calling Christianity a 'deadly superstition' — because it was, after all, a comparative newcomer to the Roman Empire. But his ignorance of Jewish history is less excusable. He derives their name from Ida in Crete, and says 'they were led out of Egypt by their chieftains Hierosolymus and Juda. They consecrated an image of an ass in their temple because a herd of asses had disclosed to them copious springs of water in their wanderings; these wanderings lasted six days; on the seventh they obtained possession of the land, where they built their city and temple.'

And the point of special interest is: Tacitus states that *'most authors agree'* that this is a true account of the Jews' origin! Evidently he failed to escape the infection of the intellectual atmosphere in which he lived. Are modern scholars more successful?

CHAPTER TWENTY-FOUR

Ancient Scoffers and Modern Scholars

'Wherever I have in this book plainly and roundly inveighed against error . . . with vehement expressions; I have done it neither out of malice nor any vainglory, but of mere necessity to vindicate the spotless truth from an ignominious bondage.'

John Milton

So far as we know, the first person to impugn the authenticity of Daniel was a Greek philosopher, Porphyry (233–304 A.D.). Notice that he lived more than 300 years after the book of Maccabees (see Appendix) was written, and 800 years after Daniel. In literary criticism, as in Nature,

'Tis distance lends enchantment to the view'

of implausible hypotheses. Doubts concerning the authorship of a book increase in direct proportion to the number of years that separate the doubter from the author. 'Was Lord Bacon the author of Shakespeare's plays?' appeared in 1856, 240 years after Shakespeare's death, and aroused some interest. It is doubtful whether a similar interest would have been evinced if the book had been published in 1656.

Why did Porphyry attack Daniel? Because he did not believe that God could or would reveal to man the shape of things to come. Therefore detailed predictions which appear to have come true must, in his opinion, have been written after the events, *whatever the historical evidence* as to their earlier date. Another case of, I've made up my mind: please don't confuse me with the facts.

We also note in Porphyry 'the dawning tendency to exalt the Master to the detriment of the interpretation given by his disciples — a method very effectual in disposing of the

Gospel, which has come down to us only through the apostles' (Pressensé). The difference is that Porphyry attacked Christianity from outside the Church, whereas many moderns do the same from within. And it was reserved for the 20th century to invent the 'pious-fraud-encourages-the-persecuted' theory. We may safely say that anyone who had actually seen Christians under fire — as Porphyry may well have done during the great persecution of 250 A.D. — would never have dreamed up such a fantasy.

Another interesting character is Celsus (178 A.D.), a sworn foe of Christianity, whom we know solely through the treatise written by Origen in refutation of his book *True Doctrine.* Celsus argued that 'the miracles are insufficiently attested; the Virgin Birth covers a story of illegitimacy; the resurrection hangs on the testimony of an hysterical female.' (Where have we heard all this before?) Most interesting of all, in the context of our present enquiry, he 'considered that the different Gospels were incorrect revisions of one original' (BFW, Canon, p. 405) which some believers remodelled and remoulded in various ways in order to answer objectors. To which Origen replies: *'I know of no people who remodel the Gospel except the followers of Marcion* and the followers of Valentinus and perhaps those of Lucan.'

It is not difficult to discern the spirit of Celsus resurrected e.g. in our Pelican Commentary which alleges that scores of verses have been altered, transposed, inserted or remodelled... in the interests of Church needs or notions or apologetics.

Finally let us take a look at Marcion (100—170 A.D.?). Son of a Bishop, he gave the early Church more trouble, perhaps, than anyone else of that era. Though regarding himself as a Christian, he rejected all the Gospels except Luke and mutilated some of Paul's epistles because 'the apostle's language did not square with Marcion's favourite tenets in all respects, and therefore he assumed that Paul's text must have been corrupted' (JBL in SR p. 273). Lecturing in Rome he succeeded in convincing many that his task was that of the expert art-dealer restoring the *original* Luke or the *original* Paul which had become overlaid with glosses, interpolations and interpretations.

All this sounds very familiar to readers of modern critical commentaries. Their claim to modernity has nothing to do with the Space Age, enlightenment, or new discoveries. It is simply the current manifestation of man's age-old dislike of God's arrangements. The scissors-and-paste Bible is but a mirror of its maker, however virtuous, and leaves unimpaired his self-will and self-esteem.

To sum up: modern Scholar is but ancient Scoffer writ large.

CHAPTER TWENTY-FIVE

The Great Classroom Con

'Let Truth and Falsehood grapple: who ever knew Truth put to the worse, in a free and open encounter?'

John Milton

Elsewhere[1] I have pointed out that the gravamen of our charge against evolution is not that it is taught, but that, knowing it to be only a theory, science teachers put it across to children as fact. Sixth formers leave school totally ignorant of the weighty scientific arguments against evolution and for creation.

Very much the same charge must be made against R.E. teachers and theologians who, knowing that there are two opposite approaches to the Bible, speak and/or write as if there were but one — and that the modernist's. This in spite of the fact that the largest Society at Cambridge University today is the Christian Union, whose doctrinal basis is 'the divine inspiration and infallibility of Holy Scripture'.

It was a sad day for British schools when the Cambridge University Press decided to end the old 'Cambridge Bible for Schools' and commissioned the new 'Cambridge Bible Commentary' to replace it. Even then, one might have hoped for some sort of balance in the presentation of different views, but we find little or none. For examples we shall look at A. W. Argyle's handling of three incidents involving Pontius Pilate:

1. his wife's dream
2. the handwashing
3. the setting of the guard

1. GBR p.91.

Argyle informs us that (1) these verses, because they do not
appear in Mark, 'may belong to the body of tradition which
Matthew derived from a Palestinian source' (of course in
Argyle's view there is no possibility of Matthew himself having
been on the spot). (2) 'may not be historical' because handwashing was a Jewish, not a Roman custom and (3) the whole
section 'is probably due to a Christian attempt to refute the
accusation of the Jews.'

The clubbing together of chief priests and Pharisees is
'hardly probable'. (Our commentator has apparently overlooked the fact that in John's Gospel they are reported as
clubbing together no less than five times against the Lord, the
last being the arrest-squad in Gethsemane). 'It also seems
improbable that the predictions of resurrection which Jesus
made privately to his disciples were known to the chief
priests and Pharisees (unless Judas had told them).'

By contrast, Carr's comments (1878) on these passages are
very much to the point. We shall take them in reverse order.

3. 'It appears from this (setting of the guard) that the
priests and Pharisees understood the true import of Christ's
words, "Destroy this temple and after three days I will raise
it up", which they wilfully misrepresented to the people.'

2. 'In washing his hands Pilate followed a Jewish custom
which all would understand'.

1'. (Pilate's wife) 'Claudia Procula: traditions state she was a
proselyte . . . which is by no means unlikely, as many of the
Jewish proselytes were women. By an imperial regulation
provincial governors had been prohibited from taking their
wives with them. But the rule gradually fell into disuse, and
an attempt made in the Senate (21 A.D.) completely failed.
(Tacitus, Annals III, 33, 34).'

To sum up the difference between the Cambridge Bible for
Schools, 1878, and the Cambridge Bible Commentary, 1973:
Carr produces historical and scriptural evidence confirming the
truth of Matthew's narrative; Argyle, without evidence, contrives to throw gratuitous doubt on all these 'additions' and
at the same time gratuitous reproach upon the Christians of
Palestine for forging lies to damn the Jews. The sixth former
who soaks up this sort of teaching will carry to university a

head stuffed with sceptical fancies but largely ignorant of historical fact. Is this sound education?

Conclusion

The great need of the hour is to produce a new conservative-evangelical commentary series specially written for O and A levels; *or* to reprint the old *Cambridge Bible for Schools*. No one who has not read these can imagine how immensely superior they are to the current *Cambridge Bible Commentary*. A few additional notes is all they need to bring them up to date.

We advocate no head-in-the-sand obscurantism. Every real difficulty should be squarely faced. But we claim *the pupil's right to make his own decision* about the authenticity of Scripture, after studying *all the facts*.

We denounce as unethical the one-sided presentation of views which are held only by a minute percentage of the world-wide Christian Church; and the deliberate withholding from children of vital information — the massive weight of evidence which supports the traditional authorship and absolute truthfulness of Matthew, Mark, Luke and John.

We conclude with one more example of contrasting comments on the same verse, Mark 13:31:

'Heaven and earth shall pass away; but My words shall not pass away'.

Cambridge Bible for Schools, 1883:

'Never did the Speaker seem to stand more utterly alone than when He made this majestic utterance. Never did it seem more improbable that it should be fulfilled. But as we look across the centuries we see how it has been realised. His words have passed into laws, they have passed into doctrines, they have passed into proverbs . . . but they have never 'passed away'. What human teacher ever dared to claim an eternity for his words?'

Pelican Commentary, 1977:

'. . . an absolute claim hardly paralleled outside St. John's Gospel, and most commentators believe it to be an early

Christian claim on Jesus' behalf — perhaps an adaptation of his saying about the Law (Matthew 5:18) to his own teaching.'

Our comment:

It's unbelievable what you have to believe if you're not a believer!

Is the Book of Daniel a Pious Fraud?

'The Biblical critics, whatever reconstructions they devise, can never be crudely proved wrong. St. Mark is dead. When they meet St. Peter there will be more pressing matters to discuss.'

C. S. Lewis, 'Fern-seed and Elephants'

Professor Nineham's assault on the integrity of Mark 13 is launched (as we have seen — chapter 22) from the platform of the assumed non-integrity of Daniel.[1] If Daniel was written 400 years after the events which it professes to foretell (so the prophecies are history-written-backward), why should not Mark 13 be another pious fraud on the same model?

So it will be pertinent to glance briefly at the arguments for the historicity of Daniel, which *appears* to have been written at Babylon in the 6th century B.C. If it can be shown that these arguments are sound, Nineham's hypothesis regarding Mark 13 will be seen to be correspondingly flimsy.

1. In the O.T. Apocrypha we find two books called Maccabees. The first 'supplies a detailed and accurate record of the years 175—135 B.C. . . . the book is one of the most precious historical sources we possess . . . it bears on its face the stamp of genuineness' (EB). In chapter 2 we read of a hero named Mattathias who revolted against the heathen king Antiochus Epiphanes. Before dying he blessed his five sons and exhorted them to follow the example of the O.T. patriarchs and prophets:

---

1. Unfortunately this myth has been perpetuated by the *Good News Bible* in the Introduction to Daniel, and also by the omission of his Name from the historical chart in the end papers. Another notable absentee is Jonah.

'Abraham . . . Joseph . . . Phineas . . . Joshua . . . Caleb
. . . David . . . Elijah for being zealous and fervent for the
law, was taken up to heaven. *Ananias, Azarias and Misael,*
by believing were saved out of the flame. *Daniel for his
innocency* was delivered from the mouth of lions. And thus
consider ye throughout all ages, that none that put their
trust in Him shall be overcome.'

Notice that Daniel and friends are bracketed with
undoubtedly historical figures; and the miracles recorded in
Daniel 3 and 6 are referred to as *undoubted historical facts.*
Now I Maccabees was written not later than 100–90 B.C., and
the date assigned to Daniel by Nineham et al. is 160 B.C.; so
only two generations separate the two books. Yet we are
asked to believe that in the course of those 60 years the
whole Jewish nation was hoodwinked into accepting Daniel
the forgery as Daniel the history! Not only so, but since (on
this hypothesis) Mattathias must have been dying about the
same time as 'Daniel' was being *written* (i.e. around 160 B.C.),
his words about fire and lions must be completely fictitious.
For who would bracket the hero of a novel written yesterday,
so to speak, with national heroes honoured for a thousand
years and more ('Boadicea, the Black Prince, Wellington,
Montgomery, *James Bond* . . .')? So we are forced to assume,
if Nineham's hypothesis be true, that the author of Maccabees
made up the words about Daniel and Friends and put them
into the mouth of Mattathias, *knowing* them to be false.
Fiction piled upon fiction, forgery upon forgery! Believe it if
you can.

If, on the other hand, we accept that in Mattathias' day
the book of Daniel had been part of the Jewish Scriptures for
350 years, all is explained. Nothing could be more natural
than to refer to chapters 3 and 6 as famous deliverances
wrought by God, *real* events to encourage people *really*
suffering under another tyrant.

2. Our second group of arguments is supplied by Josephus,
the Jewish historian who wrote 80–100 A.D. Though (obviously) not infallible, he is generally reliable except where his
own personal fortunes were concerned. Joseph Scaliger (1540–
1609), the greatest European scholar of his day, reckoned

that Josephus is more trustworthy than all Greek and Roman historians; and modern scholars quote him frequently. What does Josephus have to say about Daniel?

a. He tells the whole story of Daniel as *history*.

b. He sketches the prophecies of Daniel and concludes:

'. . . and indeed it so came to pass that our nation suffered these things under Antiochus Epiphanes, according to Daniel's vision, and what *he wrote many years before they came to pass*. In the very same manner Daniel also wrote concerning the Roman government, and that our country should be made desolate by them. *All these things did this man leave in writing,* as God had showed them to him, insomuch that they who read his prophecies and see how they have been fulfilled, would wonder at the honour wherewith God honoured Daniel.' Again, Josephus refers to Daniel as 'one of the greatest of the prophets . . . for he did not only prophesy of future events but he also determined the *time* of their accomplishment.'

c. Josephus relates that Alexander the Great came to Jerusalem on his victorious march down to Egypt (332 B.C.) — 'And when the book of Daniel was shown to him, in which Daniel declared that one of the Greeks should destroy the empire of the Persians, he supposed that he himself was the person intended.'

There are no good grounds for doubting this story. Josephus had access to scores of documents and histories which have been lost to us, and no one doubts the similar story of Alexander's visit to the temple of Ammon (Egypt) in the same year.

d. Josephus also wrote a treatise 'Against Apion' to prove that Jewish history was more accurate than Greek history. One paragraph is particularly important as showing the *date of the closing of the O.T. canon:*

'We have among us only 22 books, which contain the record of all the past times, which are justly believed to be divine; and of them five belong to Moses, which contain his laws and the traditions of the origin of mankind until his death. This interval of time was little short of 3000 years; but as to the time from the death of Moses *till the reign of*

Artaxerxes (died 424 B.C.), king of Persia, who reigned after Xerxes, the prophets . . . wrote down what was done in their times in 13 books.

It is true our history has been written since Artaxerxes, very particularly, *but has not been esteemed of the like authority with the former* by our forefathers, because there has not been an exact succession of prophets since that time . . . *no one has been so bold as to add anything to* (those 22 books) *or take anything from them, or to make any change in them;* but it becomes natural to all Jews, from their very birth, to esteem those books to contain divine doctrines, and to persist in them, and, if occasion be, willingly to die for them.'

From these words we see that Josephus considered the canon of the O.T. to have been closed by 400 B.C., and books like I and II Maccabees were 'not of like authority'. Positively this confirms his opinion previously stated in (a), (b) and (c). Negatively, it shows that the Jews would have thrown out as uncanonical any book written in 160 B.C. From every angle it is indisputable that Josephus regarded the book of Daniel as true history written in the 6th century by the prophet himself.

The fire-walkers' song

Bishop Westcott has pointed out that the history of the O.T. Canon runs parallel with the history of the N.T. Canon, as might be expected. In both cases, before the Canon was finally settled, a number of 'fringe' books were discussed and either accepted or rejected. Thus Eusebius tells us that in his day the Epistles of Barnabas and Clement were still 'disputed'. Though recognised as useful, they were (of course) finally excluded from the N.T. Canon. Similarly the 'Song of the Three Children' was recognised as a fine piece of religious poetry and has won a place in our Prayer Book as the 'Benedicite'. Written in Greek in the 3rd or 2nd century B.C. in Egypt, it purports to be a song sung by Ananias Azarias and Misael while in Nebuchadnezzar's furnace; and was added to the Greek translation of Daniel in the LXX. But from the first it was recognised as apocryphal; it had never been written in Hebrew (or Aramaic). On the other hand the 12

Hebrew/Aramaic chapters of Daniel were never disputed, never on the 'fringe'. As our four Gospels were accepted always and everywhere by all Christians, so the book of Daniel was accepted as authentic by all Jews everywhere and always.[1]

Conclusion

If 'Daniel' was a fraud foisted upon the Jewish nation by a cunning deceiver unknown to history, it is a phenomenon unique in the world's literature. No parallel can be adduced from any age or land, for a book claiming to have been written 350 years earlier suddenly appearing out of *nowhere* and being *immediately* welcomed by a *whole nation* as literal historical truth. To believe this is to believe in a miracle no less marvellous than the prophecies concerning Antiochus Epiphanes. But for the accuracy of these there is an efficient cause — the omniscience of God; whereas the 'anonymous-pious-fraud-to-comfort-the-persecuted' idea seems rather less credible than the Book of Mormon's claim to direct provenance from Heaven.

We conclude, then, that just as Genesis sets no precedent for a myth-interpretation of Matthew 1–2, so Daniel 11 sets no precedent for a prophecy-after-the-event interpretation of Mark 13. Professor Nineham like Robinson, has built his house upon sand.

1. The orthodox critical theory of Daniel's late date has taken a hammering in recent years from J. C. Whitcomb's *'Darius the Mede'*, R. K. Harrison's *'Introduction to the O.T.'* (Tyndale), and the commentaries of H. Leupold (Evangelical Press, 1973) and Joyce Baldwin (IVP, 1977). It would be outside the scope of this book to attempt a summary of their excellent arguments. The quotations from Josephus are given at length because some A level R.E. textbooks *do not even mention his views* or Mattathias' words. This seems to me deplorable. I believe students have a right to know *all* the evidence on *both* sides of a disputed topic.

The Authenticity of the Gospels

Proposition: The four Gospels were written respectively by Matthew and John, Apostles; by Mark the companion of Peter and Luke the companion of Paul.

General Evidence

A. Presumptive Evidence from the Old Testament:

1. God chooses holy men for His revelations: II Peter 1:21; Jeremiah 1:4, 5.

2. God commits their writings to His people: Deuteronomy 31:9; Romans 3:2; II Timothy 3:15;

B. Internal Evidence from the New Testament:

Christ chose the Apostles and prepared them

1. By a unique appointment: Mark 3:14; Matthew 16:18; Luke 22:28—30. cf. Ephesians 2:20; Revelations 21:14; I Corinthians 9:1—2; I John 1:1—3.

2. By a unique assignment: John 15:27; 17—18 (*only* Apostles, cp. v. 20); Luke 24:48; Acts 1:8, 22; 10:41; I Peter 5:1;

3. By a unique equipment:
   a. perfect interpretation of the O.T. Luke 24:44—45; Acts 1:3.
   b. perfect memorisation: John 14:26.
   c. perfect revelation: John 15:15; 16:13.

Particular Evidence: Matthew

A. External Evidence for Matthew's authorship of the first Gospel.

1. *Origen*[1]: 'Concerning the Gospels, which alone are uncontroverted in the Church of God spread under heaven, I have learnt by tradition that that according to Matthew, who was once a publican but afterwards an apostle of Jesus Christ, was written first . . .'

2. *Justin Martyr:* '. . . for the apostles in the memoirs made by them, which are called Gospels, handed down that it was thus enjoined on them . . .'

3. *Irenaeus:* 'Matthew brought out a writing of the Gospel . . .'

4. *Tertullian:* '. . . the authority of the apostolic churches will uphold the other Gospels . . . I mean those of Matthew and John.

5. *Papias:* 'Matthew composed the Logia in Hebrew; and each one translated them as he was able.'

B. What does 'logia' mean?

1. Originally 'logia' meant 'words spoken by God' (Acts 7:38; I Peter 4:11).

2. But in the N.T. *part* of the O.T. is often named instead of the whole (Matthew 5:17; Luke 24:27, 44; Romans 3:19).

3. We do the same today in calling our 27 books 'the New Testament' although the words occur in 11 books only.

This is a common figure of speech, 'synecdoche' = part for the whole.

4. Paul uses 'logia' in this way in Romans 3:2, obviously referring to the whole O.T.

5. The Jewish philosopher Philo (40 A.D.) quotes Genesis 4: 15(b) as an oracle (logion) of the Lord. This (second) half of the verse is *not* a quotation of God's words but a narrative of His *action* ('the Lord appointed a sign . . .').

6. Clement of Rome (96 A.D.) uses the word 'logia' as equivalent to Scripture.

7. Eusebius, who quotes Papias' words (A.5, above), certainly

---

1. For biographical notes on the Church Fathers see pp. 135—140.

understood him to be speaking of the *Gospel,* since Eusebius had just before quoted Papias' comments on the origin of Mark's Gospel.

8. Papias (on Mark) practically defines his own use of the word, since he speaks of the 'kuriaka logia' as 'that which was either said *or done* by Christ'. (see p. 135)

C. Why then did not Papias say, 'Matthew composed the Gospel'?

1. In Papias' day the word 'gospel' had not yet come to be applied generally to the *books.* Even now it is absent from our oldest Mss. cp. Justin (150 A.D.): '. . . the apostles in the memoirs made by them, *which are called gospels.'*
The word required explanation 25 years after Papias wrote.

2. If Papias had used the word 'scripture' to denote the book, it would have seemed to make Christ himself the author (i.e. 'the Lord's writing').

3. Papias therefore used *the only word* which would show at once two things:
    a. that the Lord was the *subject* of the book, not its author.
    b. that in regard to its authority the book was on a level with the Old Testament.

Conclusion.

Therefore we may safely paraphrase Papias' quotation as follows:

    'Matthew composed the Gospel (which has the same authority as Scripture) in Hebrew . . .'

D. The language of the first Gospel

The Problem:

1. Early Christian writers say that Matthew wrote in Hebrew for Palestinian Jews.

2. but they also quote the Gospel in Greek and regard Matthew as its author.

3. All scholars agree that the Gospel is not a translation.

A Possible Solution:

1. Matthew was bi-lingual. As a civil servant of the Roman Empire, he probably had to be.

2. He wrote first in Hebrew for Palestinian Jews, then in Greek for all Christians.
    N.B. Josephus did the same with his 'Wars of the Jews'.

3. Papias probably meant: 'Greek-speaking Jews/Christians used to have difficulty in understanding Matthew's Hebrew Gospel; but now that we have it in Greek, no translation is required.'

4. The Hebrew version has apparently been lost. After the destruction of Jerusalem (70 A.D.) it would have been little in demand.

E. Internal evidence that Matthew wrote the Gospel

1. The title — 'kata MATTHAION'
    a. is on every MS we possess. There is no evidence that the book ever existed without it.
    b. it distinguishes the message of Matthew from the message of (e.g.) Malachi:
        the prophet had a burden to deliver
        the apostle had a person to depict;
        the prophet wrote from inward intuition
        the apostle wrote from outward observation.
    c. it links the message of Matthew with the message of Mark, Luke and John.

ONE gospel — ONE Lord.

If he had written 'the Gospel *of* Matthew, some might have thought it was a message of doctrine peculiar to Matthew. Cp. I Corinthians 15:11.

d. it constitutes a claim to authorship of the writing but not of the message.

Compare Romans 8:27 in the NEB: 'kata Theon' = 'in God's own way'. Therefore we may safely paraphrase 'kata Matthaion' as 'the Gospel of Jesus Christ presented in Matthew's own way'.

OBJECTION:

'kata' (= according to) means only 'in the style of' or 'as we heard it from'.

ANSWER:

1. It is admitted by all that the second Gospel is 'according to' Peter's teaching.

2. therefore if 'kata' means only 'as we heard it from', the 2nd Gospel would certainly have been designated 'kata Petron'.

3. but it is *not* 'kata Petron', it is 'kata Markon'.

4. therefore 'kata' must denote authorship, not merely a vague connection.

5. therefore the title 'kata Matthaion' means

Matthew wrote this book

2. His *MODESTY:*

1. Compare 9:9—10 with Luke 5:27—29.
   a. there is no mention of him 'leaving all'
   b. nor of Matthew himself giving the feast.

2. 10:3 with Luke 6:15.
   a. his name is put after Thomas
   b. Matthew calls himself 'publican', a word of ignominy.

3. His special interest in *MONEY:*

1. 10:9; 2:11; 23:16, 17 (only in Matthew is gold mentioned).

2. Temple tax — 17:24 ff.

3. Parables —
   a. Unforgiving Servant, ch. 18
   b. Labourers in the Vineyard, ch. 20
   c. Talents (especially 'bankers' — 25:27).

4. *MISTAKE*

The quotation from Zechariah in 27:9 is referred to Jeremiah. It is very hard to see how this apparently erroneous reference could have survived in our manuscripts *unless* the original had apostolic authority and therefore the early copyists *dare* not change it. (The explanation offered in JFB Commentary seems as good as any). A possible parallel in our A.V. is the retention of 'strain *at* a gnat' (Matthew 23:24) instead of 'strain *out*'. A mistake was made, the mistake became 'authorised', so the mistake had to be retained.

SUMMARY

1. The internal evidence is suggestive: Matthew *could* have written the Gospel.

2. The external evidence is decisive: all writers of the early Church agree that Matthew *did* write the Gospel.

   But what do the critics say?
Vincent Taylor (1960): 'The view that Matthew the apostle wrote the first Gospel is now almost universally abandoned.'

F. *Objections to Matthew's authorship*

I. 'Defects' of the Gospel:
   a. time and place are vague
   b. descriptions are dull (e.g. compared 8:28 with Mark 5: 1–5), 'therefore it is not the work of an eye-witness'.

ANSWER

1. Matthew had a personality very different from Peter's.

  Peter: fisherman, bold, extrovert. His style is rough, vivid, unpolished.

  Matthew: civil servant, well-educated, retiring; polished style, restrained.

2. The Jews (for whom Matthew wrote) were very different from the Romans. Their greatest men were *prophets*, therefore Matthew lays stress on Jesus' character as the great Prophet and Preacher. Roman heroes were men of *action*, so to them Jesus is set forth as the mighty *Worker*.

3. Matthew had to condense his narrative to make room for more teaching, as follows:

	Narrative	*Teaching*
Matthew	25% (7 chs.)	75%
Mark	50% (8 chs.)	50%

But Matthew has additional narrative not in Mark:

Nativity + Temptation	2 chs.
Miracles etc.	1 ch.
total extra	3 chs.

therefore narrative in Matthew covering same stories in Mark = 7 − 3 = 4 chapters

therefore Matthew had to put into 4 chapters what Mark puts into 8, i.e. he had to 'boil down' the narrative by 50%.

4. Matthew writing for Jews in Judaea had no need to give much historical setting, e.g. compare Matthew 15 with Mark 7. Matthew omits vv. 3—4 of Mark.

II. 'superfluities':

  a. Nativity story
  b. Resurrection of the saints (27:51)
  c. Peter walking on water (14:29).

The reasoning behind this argument appears to be:

  apostles told the truth,
  these miraculous events cannot be true,
therefore no apostle wrote these things. Q.E.D.

ANSWER

The miracle of the Resurrection must include and confirm all lesser/other miracles reported by the same Evangelist.

(N.B. All scholars agree that the Gospel is a literary unity, having *one* author).

III. 'Improbability':

    an apostle would never have copied from a non-apostle (i.e. Mark).

Premise: the author of the first Gospel copied from Mark.
Conclusion: therefore the author was not an apostle.

ANSWER:

A. Repetition does not exclude inspiration.

    Compare I Kings 10 with II Chronicles 9; II Samuel 22 with Psalm 18,

therefore even if we had Mark's exact words + the Nativity story, Sermon on the Mount, etc. we could still accept it as the work of an apostle.

B. But in fact it is certain that 'Matthew did *not* copy from Mark:

1. The theory is *chronologically improbable*. External evidence is all against it:

    a. Irenaeus: 'Matthew published a writing of the Gospel while Peter and Paul went westward and founded the Church in Rome. But after the departure (= death ?) of these, Mark delivered to us in writing the things which were preached by Peter.'

    b. Clement of Alexandria: '. . . those Gospels were written first which have the genealogies.'

    c. Origen: '. . . that according to Matthew was written first . . .'

    d. In all MSS, Matthew heads the four Gospels.

2. The theory that 'Matthew' copied Mark is *verbally unprovable*.

    a. Greek admits of far more variety than English:

i.   In word order. e.g. 'the man is good' can be translated in six different ways using the same four Greek words.

ii.   In vocabulary, e.g. different words are used for 'consider' in Matthew 6:28 and Luke 12:27. (Even the Revised Version of 1881, which usually tries to reproduce in the English verbal distinctions of the Greek, has failed here).

iii.   In tenses, e.g. weak and strong Aorist, compare Matthew 23:37 with Luke 13:34. There is no possible way of reproducing this distinction in English (see Part I p. 52).

therefore in 'parallel' sections of our Gospels the verbal coincidences (= same words in the same order) are far fewer than the English translation suggests.

Without a knowledge of Greek it is impossible to form any sound judgment on the Synoptic Problem.

Dean Alford writes (Greek N.T., 1850): 'In no one case does any Evangelist borrow from another any considerable part of even a single narrative.'

b. Examples to show that Matthew could not have copied from Mark

	Withered Hand (12:9=3:1)	Sower (13:18=4:18)	Transfiguration (17:1=9:2)
(First figure denotes chapter in Matthew, second in Mark)			
Matthew's words	90	128	232
Mark's words	94	143	208
Words common in both	26	32	102
Longest common sentence	4 words	7	10

Note: i. These remarkably consistent results, which could be paralleled anywhere else in the two Gospels, show that not more than 5% of words alleged to have been 'copied' are actually the same in the same order.

ii. The longest common sentence out of 500 verses supposed to have been 'taken from Mark' is found in Matthew 16:24 = Mark 8:35. Even here the beginning and ending of the two verses are different.

c. *Challenge:* compare any passage in Mark with the corresponding passage in Matthew. Very rarely will *any* sentence exactly similar be found longer than ten words.

d. What about Aramaic?
Answer: no one has yet dared to suggest that Mark wrote in Aramaic for Greek-speaking Romans.

So what 'Matthew' borrowed from Mark, he must have borrowed in *Greek*.

Conclusion:
If 'Matthew' borrowed from Mark, he has deliberately changed Mark's word-order, vocabulary, grammar and syntax *for no conceivable purpose*! (see pp. 61/2)

3. The theory that Matthew copied from Mark is psychologically impossible.

a. The Jews firmly believed in the verbal inspiration of their Scriptures. (see pp. 97/8)
b. The early Church regarded Mark as Holy Scripture on a level with the Old Testament.
c. Therefore a Jew who wished to include part of Mark in his own version would never have dared to alter it as Matthew has 'altered' Mark.

The last twelve verses of Mark

A. *Preliminary Remarks*: right perspective.
1. The authorship of these verses is much less important than that of Matthew or John. Nearly everything here is repeated in other Gospels or Acts.

2. There is good Scriptural precedent for an Epilogue being written by another hand, e.g. Deuteronomy, Job.

3. Therefore even if it were proved beyond doubt that Mark did not write them, we would not need to reject them as unhistorical or uninspired.

4. It is practically certain that Mark cannot have intended to conclude at v. 8.
He is the only Evangelist who calls his book a 'Gospel', yet the only one who omits the Good News!

Compare I Corinthians 15:5–8 and Acts 2:32. Paul and Peter stress not the testimony of angels but the Lord's appearances.

B. *External Evidence*

Against their authenticity	*For* their authenticity
Codex Sinaiticus (350 A.D.) Codex Vaticanus (350 A.D.)	The same scribe wrote both MSS and left a space where the verses could have been. It seems that their omission was deliberate.

Against their authenticity	*For* their authenticity
Very few Greek MSS	95% of Greek MSS include them.
Versions: Armenian (10th century) Arabic (10th century) One Latin (4th century)	All other versions (from 150 A.D.). Vulgate
Jerome 406 (doubts)	Jerome 415
Eusebius 320 (doubts)	Justin Martyr 160
	Irenaeus 180 (quotes v.19 as Mark's)
	Tatian 180

C. *Internal difficulties and their answer*

1. *Difference* in style of these verses as compared with the rest.

Answer: style depends on subject, manner depends on matter.

In 1:1 — 16:8 Mark tells a story, in 16:9—20 he writes a precis (cp. his account of the Temptation in 1:13: 40 days compressed into one verse).

2. *Differences* in vocabulary.

Dean Alford: '21 words and expressions in these verses, never used elsewhere by Mark'.

Answer: Canon Cook: '. . . but the same proportion of peculiar words and expressions are found in all sections of the Gospel which are peculiar to Mark (i.e. 39 in 20 vv.)'.
Example: the parable in 4:26—29 is found only in Mark. It has 9 'peculiar words and expressions' but no one rejects the parable because of them.

D. *Internal Harmonies*

The last twelve verses (LTV) contain 5 typically Marcan features:

1. emphasis on the expulsion of devils (23 times in Mark, 9 in Matthew).
2. emphasis on the unbelief of the apostles. Compare 4:40; 6:52; 8:17.

3. the phrase 'the gospel' (without 'of the kingdom' etc.) is peculiar to Mark (1:1, 15; 8:35; 10:29; 13:10; 14:9; 16:15).

4. the word for 'sick' (5 times in the NT, 3 in Mark).

5. the word 'creation' (thrice in Mark, never in Matthew, Luke or John).

E. *Alternative theory:*

'The L.T.V. were written by a catechist who had read Matthew, Luke, John and Acts and rounded off the 'mutilated' Gospel with a potted version of his own.'

Objections to this theory

I. There are 4 unmistakable signs of the writer's independence:
   1. v. 11 is not stated in John 20:10.
   2. v. 13 seems to contradict Luke 24:34.
   3. v. 14 is very much stronger than Luke 24:36—43.
   4. the promise re poison is unique in the N.T. and has no recorded fulfilment. It is most unlikely that it would have been inserted by a third-generation Christian after the miracles had largely ceased.

II. How did the writer contrive, 30—40 years after the publication of Mark 1—16:8, to have his potted version inserted into 98% of all the MSS circulating[1] throughout the Roman Empire? Remember, in those days there was no 1st edition, 2nd edition etc. emanating from one source, as books are published today. If the first 100 copies carried a mistake, that mistake (or omission) would inevitably have been reproduced in the next 1000 copies. Before the invention of printing, the launching of a book was as irrevocable as the launching of a space-rocket. This seems to be a strong argument for judging the *majority* of MSS, rather than the minority, to represent the original.

III. Irenaeus, who had lived in Asia Minor, Rome and Gaul, unhesitatingly quotes 16:19 as Mark's. How could he be mistaken?

1. (If the 'catechist' had read John's Gospel (see I. 1. above) he could not have written earlier than 100 A.D. i.e. at least 30 years after the publication of Mark 1—16:8. By that time thousands of copies must have been in circulation.

F. *Conclusion*

The most probable explanation seems to be that the L.T.V. were written by Mark himself, rounding off the Gospel (perhaps after Peter's death) with a precis in his own words of the Resurrection appearances which he had heard of inside the apostolic circle in Jerusalem.

* * *

Over the past 100 years the authenticity of these verses has been defended by not a few scholars, including

1. J. W. Burgon (1871), *The Last Twelve Verses of the Gospel according to St. Mark.* This book is still in print in America (Sovereign Grace Book Club) and an excellent summary can be obtained for 25p from Bishop D. A. Thompson, 7 Ashley Drive, Walton-on-Thames, Surrey KT12 1JL.

2. George Salmon, Regius Professor of Divinity, Dublin University (1885):

'In spite of the eminence of the critics who reject the 12 verses, I cannot help looking at them as having been from the first an integral part of the Second Gospel.'

(Dr. Salmon was also a brilliant mathematician and a Fellow of the Royal Society).

3. Dr. Campbell Morgan (1930), Minister of Westminster Chapel:

'While recognising the difficulties giving rise to the contention, I most strongly hold that they are certainly genuine, the weight of evidence both external and internal compelling me to that conclusion.'

4. Monsignor Ronald Knox in his translation of the Bible (1963):

'. . . these last twelve verses . . . are evidently a primitive account and there is no reason why we should not ascribe their inclusion here to St. Mark.'

5. W. R. Farmer (*The Last Twelve Verses of Mark*, 1974, Cambridge University Press). After a very careful and scholarly investigation he concludes that, on balance, the evidence both

internal and external argues for the inclusion of these verses as part of the original Gospel.

It is therefore somewhat surprising to read Professor Nineham's claim in our Pelican Commentary:

'. . . the R.S.V. is *certainly* right in treating these verses as spurious . . . *all* scholars concur in this view'!

Luke and Mark

The theory that Luke used Mark's Gospel is

a. *Chronologically improbable*

1. The reasons for dating Acts in 62/63 A.D. are over-whelming and are accepted by nearly all Bible-believing scholars (and some others). Therefore Luke's Gospel must have been written before or during Paul's first imprisonment in Rome, i.e. 59—61 A.D.

2. Unanimous tradition of the early Church states that Mark's Gospel was written during or after Peter's ministry in Rome, i.e. 64—66 A.D.

b. *Psychologically improbable*

1. It is unlikely that Luke should class Mark's Gospel as one of the 'many attempts' (1:1) to which he refers, and presume to supersede it by his own.

2. It is even less likely that he should dare to chop and change that Gospel, knowing it to possess apostolic authority.

c. *Verbally unprovable,* as the following table will show:

Resurrection story		Parliamentary Report 19 Feb. 1964	
Luke's words	121	*Glasgow Herald*	144
Mark's words	136	*The Times*	156
Words in common	26 (=20%)	Words in common	36 (=24%)
Longest common sentence	3 words	Longest common sentence	6 words

Note: i. The identical words are no more than you would expect when the same events are recorded by different eye-witnesses for different types of reader.

ii. It is preposterous to infer that the *Herald* reporter copied from *The Times*. It is equally preposterous to infer that Luke copied from Mark.

iii. The identical words in speech can easily be explained by oral tradition (see below).

Further Examples:

	Sower Parable	Olivet Discourse
Mark	151	280
Luke	90	266
Words in common	37 (= 31%)	88 (= 32%)
Longest common sentence	7 words	11 words

Challenge:

As for Matthew and Mark (p. 109), compare any passage in Mark with the corresponding passage in Luke. Very rarely will any sentence exactly similar be found longer than 10 words.

Conclusion

It is in the highest degree improbable that Luke used Mark as a 'source'. No sane person would have thus chopped and changed word-order, vocabulary, tenses, prepositions and syntax — all adding up to *no significant change whatever in meaning* (see chapter 17).

Matthew, Luke and 'Q'

The idea that Matthew and Luke used a common written source Q is widely accepted by scholars today. Against this theory we may set the following:

1. Matthew the apostle would never have *needed* to depend on written sources, since he had heard the Lord's words himself and had repeated them hundreds of times in the course of his ministry at Jerusalem.

2. Luke does not *acknowledge* any written sources. His preface (1:1—4) implies that he received his information direct from eye-witnesses who were also preachers of the 'word'.

3. Some scholars believe that the 'logia' referred to by Papias (see p. 102) were not Matthew's Gospel but this 'Q' document, and that 'logia' must mean 'direct communications from God' (i.e. excluding narrative). But when we turn to the passages

common to Matthew and Luke we find the following distribution of words in the first two sections (Luke 3:7—9, 15—17; 4:1—13):

Narrative	115 words
John the Baptist	117
Christ	25
Satan	75
Total	332

So in fact the 'direct communication from God' (i.e. Christ's words) form only 7% of the whole!

4. If the 'logia' were written in Hebrew and Matthew and Luke translated them independently (Papias implies there was no authorised Greek version), it is hard to account for the longer common sentences (Luke 7:8; 9:58; 10:21; 22; 11:9, 10, 32; 12:46; 16:13). The odds against such long identical sentences being produced by independent translators are very long indeed.

5. In fact all scholars agree that these parallels must come from a Greek original (oral or written). In other words they postulate for Q exactly what we postulate for Matthew's Gospel, namely

    a. that the word 'logia' does not exclude narrative,
    b. that at some time an authorised Greek equivalent of the 'logia' must have been published, though we do not know by whom (see p. 104).

6. This is exactly the position of the early Church Fathers vis-a-vis Matthew's Gospel: they all say he wrote it in Hebrew, they all quote from it in Greek.

7. Even modern scholars admit that Eusebius thought Papias was referring to Matthew's *Gospel*. The early Church Fathers know nothing of any other document written by him.

8. Q. is not what it is supposed to be. If we add up all the words which T. W. Manson (a noted modern scholar) lumps together as Q, the total is 4313. But of these only 1511 are *actually common* to Matthew and Luke. The remaining 2802, though parallel in meaning, are in fact different Greek words. So once again we are faced with the question: why should any

sane person let alone a Christian writer, chop and change two thirds of a valuable document *to no purpose whatever?*

'Q' Examined in detail

A. The theory confounds and confuses things which differ:

1. To say that Luke 6:20 = Matthew 5:3
                    Luke 6:21 = Matthew 5:6
is to make nonsense of language.

2. The sending of the Twelve into the cities of Israel is equated with the sending of the Seventy into every city (Matthew 10: 6, 23; Luke 10).

3. Luke 12:2 = Matthew 10:26 is used in Luke as a warning against hypocrisy, in Matthew as an encouragement to preaching. Yet the passages are said to be parallel!

4. The denunciation of the Pharisees in a private house is equated with the denunciation in the Temple (Luke 11:37 ff, Matthew 23). (actual words in agreement: 45 out of 225)

5. Weather forecasts exactly opposite are said to be the same (Luke 12:54, 55; Matthew 16:2, 3) (agreement 4/46).

6. The lament over Jerusalem is said to have been spoken only once, although it fits both contexts perfectly (Luke 13, Matthew 23: see p. 50).

7. The parable of the Great Supper is supposed to be the same as the Wedding Feast (Luke 14, Matthew 22), though they have only one word in common in 180.

8. General predictions of the Second Coming are confounded with the Olivet Discourse (Luke 17, Matthew 24) in spite of the small verbal agreement (48/245).

B. In passages which are truly parallel, the theory of Q *fails to account for the differences,* e.g.

1. Parable of the Two Builders (Luke 6, Matthew 7): agreement 10/82.

2. Casting out devils: why 'finger' in Luke 11:20; 'Spirit' in Matthew 12:28?

3. Compare Matthew 18:6, 7 with Luke 17:1, 2: three subjects are mentioned,

   a. stumbling of little ones
   b. drowning in the sea
   c. causes of stumbling inevitable.

Matthew puts them in the order a-b-c.
Luke puts them in the order c-b-a.
Why? — if they are copying a common document.

4. Same passages in the A.V.; these words are identical — 'it were better for him that a millstone were hanged . . .' but in the Greek, five out of the six words are different. Why?

5. A striking comparison:

Centurion's Servant		Paul's Conversion	
Matthew 8	166 words	Paul (Acts 22 & 26)	88 words
Luke 7	172	Luke (Acts 9)	74
common	60 (35%)	common	28 (37%)

Note: You will remember that the story of Paul's conversion is told three times in Acts: first (presumably in private) to Luke, the narrator; secondly, on the Temple steps to a hostile mob of Jews; thirdly, in a formal defence before king Agrippa. The degree of correspondence between these three descriptions of the same event, is shown above.

Now

a. *If* we admit that in Acts 9:22 and 26 we have eyewitness reports of the same event recollected by the same person and re-told orally to different audiences with a different purpose in each case — *Then* we must also admit that the story of the Centurion's Servant could equally well have been re-told by different people (or even by the same person) to different audiences, and yet have had 35% words common to each 'telling'.

b. if it is *not* necessary to believe that the accounts of Paul's conversion in Acts 9:22, and 26 were separately copied and changed from some 'lost' document, — *so neither* is it necessary to believe that the accounts of Christ's teaching common to Matthew and Luke were copied and changed from Q or any other 'lost' document.

6. All scholars agree that Matthew's and Luke's account of the Passion and Resurrection are independent except where 'they both depend on Mark'. Therefore Q contained nothing on the Passion or Resurrection, i.e. Q was a Gospel without *the* Gospel!

Is it likely that such a document ever circulated in the early Church?

Answer

The great majority of references to Christ in Acts and the Epistles concern his Passion and Resurrection. Therefore it is highly improbable that an authorised 'Sayings Collection' lacking these vital chapters was ever allowed to circulate.

Note also that the 'attempted' narratives of Luke 1:1 concern not the teaching or discourses of the Lord but the *facts* (Greek *pragmata*) or 'things *done*'.

Conclusion

The idea of a 'Sayings Collection' from which Matthew and Luke 'copied' is a figment of the imagination of modern critics. All the evidence, external and internal, is against it.

The Synoptic Problem

I. *Why were the Gospels not written earlier?*

a. The Rabbis had a rule, 'Commit nothing to writing'.

b. The apostles probably expected the Lord to return in their lifetime (Matthew 10:23; John 21:22; Acts 1:7).

They did not know the times and seasons any more than we do, so they felt no need to write a permanent record.

c. The Old Testament was written on tables of stone: the New Testament was to be written on hearts of flesh (II Corinthians 3:3; Hebrews 8:10; I John 2:27). To make this distinction clear, a time-lag was necessary before the new law was written.

d. From 30–60 A.D. the witness of the Holy Spirit took the form of miracles (Mark 16:20; Acts; Hebrews 2:4) and direct revelations (I Corinthians 14:26).

Therefore the churches did not feel the need of written teaching.

e. The Old Testament was regarded as a storehouse of Christian truth in itself (II Timothy 3:16).

f. The apostles needed *experience* in teaching, in order to select the right incidents and reduce the 10 million words which they had heard to the 10 thousand which they recorded (see p. 4). cp. Paul did not write the epistle to the Romans till he had been preaching for (about) 20 years.

II. *Was the tradition oral or written?*

a. In all the Epistles (48—68 A.D.) there is not a single reference to a miracle or parable of Christ; in Acts and the Epistles there are only two quotations of His words (Acts 20:35; I Timothy 5:18).

b. The emphasis throughout is on *hearing:* Romans 10:14—18; Ephesians 4:21 (contrast 3:4); II Timothy 2:2; Hebrews 2:1; I John 2:7, 18, 24.

c. *Identical words are more frequent in speeches* than in the narrative, in these proportions:

Matthew 12:5
Mark 4:1
Luke 9:1

that is, for every word identical with a word in the narrative of another Gospel, Luke has nine words identical with another Gospel in *speeches*. This is easy to explain by oral tradition but very hard to explain on any documentary theory. For why should a copyist 'chop and change' more in a narrative than in a speech?

d. Analysis of Parliamentary reports in any two newspapers will show roughly the same results, e.g. of the 36 words in common in the example (p. 114), 4 coincidences occur in the narrative as against 32 in the speeches.

Why? Because *comments* will vary according to the reporter's point of view, but speeches should be reported verbatim.

Objection:

'. . . they could not have memorised the whole Gospel (e.g.) of Matthew.'

Answer:

1. Melanchton knew the whole Greek New Testament by heart.

2. Bishop Westcott knew hundreds of lines of Homer.

3. Brahmins know thousands of lines of their Shastras.

How much more would an apostle have been able to remember the words of the Son of God, helped by the Holy Spirit (John 14:26). See also p. 134.

e. *Conclusion:* Oral tradition alone can adequately explain our Gospels.

III. *How can the similarities be accounted for, without Documents?*

1. The apostles were together for about 20 years after the Ascension (Acts 8:1; 15:2, 4), every day teaching and hearing each other teach (Acts 5:42; 6:4).

2. Gradually the Holy Spirit taught them which incidents and discourses required most emphasis in this teaching.

3. As these (comparatively) few stories and speeches were repeated over and over again, they tended to become stereotyped, especially the words of Christ.

IV. *How can the differences be accounted for?*

1. Similar incidents must not be assumed to be the same (see chapter 13), e.g. the two anointings (Luke 7, Matthew 26).

2. The Lord repeated important sayings many times to different audiences, and even several times to the same people (Matthew 19:30, 20:16). cp. also the four sayings on Divorce: Matthew 5:32 = Luke 16:8
             Matthew 19:9 = Mark 10:11
and He may have spoken on this subject 40 times rather than 4.

3. General orders to the Twelve may have been modified to individual disciples, e.g. Mark 6:8, 9 with Matthew 10, Luke 9. Or it may mean: 'Don't buy a staff specially for this trip.'

V. *Summary of the Synoptic problem*

1. The basic oral tradition was formed in Jerusalem between

30 and 50 A.D. by the apostles continual preaching and teaching, winnowing and selection of incidents and discourses.

2. 'The Gospels with the genealogies were written first' (Clement of Alexandria), as follows:

    a. Matthew in Jerusalem c. 63 A.D., adding to the basic oral tradition his own personal reminiscences and those of Joseph (chapters 1–2).

    b. Luke's perhaps in Caesarea about 60 A.D., adding to the tradition Mary's reminiscences (see Part I chapter 21) and those of the 120 (Acts 1:15).

3. Mark was written at Rome c. 65 A.D. at Peter's dictation (according to Jerome), being the basic tradition plus Peter's personal reminiscences.

4. Thus Mark probably does represent most nearly the basic oral tradition (Peter's preaching, perhaps, being the model for others), but there is no reason why it should not have been *written* last of the three.

19th century scholar's view:

1. T. M. Lindsay D.D., Professor of Divinity and Church History at the Free Church College, Glasgow, 1883:

'Almost every English scholar of any eminence upholds the "oral" hypothesis, that the writers of the Synoptic Gospels made use of a common oral Gospel in which a cycle of representative facts about Jesus were described in language which had become stereotyped by use.'

Comment: Professor Lindsay includes the word 'English' because at that time German scholarship was already notorious for apostasy and rationalism.

2. Canon Farrar D.D. (Cambridge Bible for Schools) 1888 (commenting on Luke 1:1):

'It may be regarded as certain that among these "attempts" Luke did *not* class the Gospels of Matthew and Mark. The inference that he was either unaware of the existence of those Gospels, or made no direct use of them, suggests itself with the utmost force when we place side by side any of the events which they narrate in common, and mark the minute and inexplicable differences which incessantly occur even amid general similarity.'

3. Dean Alford's commentary (1850):

'It is inconceivable that one writer borrowing from another matter confessedly of the first importance, in good faith and with approval, should alter his diction so singularly and capriciously as, on this hypothesis (of copying/changing) we find the text of the parallel sections of our Gospel altered.'

The Fourth Gospel — Authorship

'The genuineness of St. John's Gospel is the centre of the position of those who uphold the historical truth of the record of our Lord Jesus Christ given us in the New Testament.

Hence the attacks of the opponents of revealed religion are concentrated upon it.'

Bishop J. B. Lightfoot, 1880

We shall make no attempt to summarise the massive, cumulative and (to my mind) decisive arguments for apostolic authorship, because they have been set out fifty times before and can be read again today in the commentaries of William Hendriksen and Leon Morris. Our main purpose here is to show how subjective and defective is the presentation given to *school*children, especially in the Cambridge Bible Commentary (1972). We shall answer Professor Hunter in the words of his predecessor, Rev. A. Plummer M.A., D.D., Master of University College, Durham, formerly Fellow and Tutor of Trinity College, Oxford, who edited the 'Cambridge Bible for Schools and Colleges' commentary on John in 1892.

Hunter:

'A second-century tradition whose chief witness is Irenaeus affirms that the Apostle John lived to a ripe old age in Ephesus and issued the Gospel there.'

(Note the first word 'A', conveying the idea of *one single story*.)

Plummer:

'When we pass beyond 170 A.D. the evidence becomes full and clear: Tatian, the Epistle to the Churches of Vienna and Lyons, Celsus, the Muratorian Fragment, Clementine

Homilies, Theophilus of Antioch, Athenagoras, Ireaeus, Clement of Alexandria, and Tertullian. Of these none perhaps is more important than Irenaeus the pupil of Polycarp who was a friend of John. It never occurs to him to maintain that the Fourth Gospel is the work of St. John; he teats it as a universally acknowledged fact.'

Hunter:

'. . . not so convincing is the case for his (John's) actual authorship . . . "he wrote it" (21:24) may mean "he caused it to be written", as it does in 19:19.'

Our comment:

We may hope that Hunter's readers will look up the reference. If they do, they can scarcely fail to see how it completely refutes the point that he is trying to make. To be sure, Pilate did not with his own hands block out the title *Jesus of Nazareth the King of the Jews,* but every word was written *at his dictation* and he refused to change even one word (or two) to please the priests. This is all we claim for any book of the N.T. John may have been blind and needing to use an amanuensis, as Paul used Tertius (Romans 16:22), but the Gospel came from his mind and mouth as surely as 'Paradise Lost' came from the mind and mouth of Milton in his blindness.

Hunter:

'The case is weakened by the fact that . . . the Alogi . . . refused to accept John's Gospel.'

Plummer:

'. . . if the Fourth Gospel was rejected in certain quarters for a time, this tells little or nothing against its genuineness. Indeed it may fairly be said to tell the other way; for it shows that the universal recognition of the Gospel, which we find existing from 170 A.D. onwards, was no blind enthusiasm but a victory of truth over baseless but not unnatural suspicion' (because it was different from Matthew-Mark-Luke).

Hunter:

'Would the apostle have been likely to style himself his

Master's "favourite pupil"?' ('the disciple whom Jesus loved').

Plummer:

'The answer is that St. John does nothing of the kind. St. Peter takes the lead in the Fourth Gospel as in the other three . . . To suppose that the phrase . . . implies self-glorification at the expense of others is altogether to misunderstand it. Rather, it is
   a. a permanent expression of gratitude
   b. a modest explanation of the prominent part he was called upon to play on certain occasions, e.g. 13:23; 19:26; 21:7.'

The worst charge against Professor Hunter is that, *knowing all that has been written* by first-class scholars in defence of the traditional view, he makes no attempt to strike a balance and allow pupils to make up their own minds. He professes to 'marshal the evidence and see where it leads us'; but in fact he selects about 10% of the evidence and *tells* us where (he thinks) that leads us:

'The solution which does best justice to all the facts is that the actual author was himself a close disciple of the Apostle John, the Beloved Disciple.'

No pupil reading that Introduction would have the faintest idea that the evidence for apostolic authorship of the Fourth Gospel is ten times stronger than for Thucydides' authorship of the *History of the Peloponnesian War* or Virgil's of the *Aeneid.* Nor is he given any inkling that many of the finest minds of Christendom, looking at *exactly the same facts,* arrived at the opposite conclusion to Hunter's — namely, that all the miracles here recorded were actual historical events, and all the words attributed to Jesus were actually spoken by Him at the time and place specified.

One personal reminiscence. While the author was teaching at Rickmansworth School the sixth form produced a magazine with an article 'Throw Away the Crutch'. This was a childish attack on Christianity, using scurrilous language and pseudo-historical arguments — including, 'John's Gospel represents the dreaming of an Asiatic mystic', or words to that effect. Who can blame the boy for repeating what he had doubtless heard taught in an R.E. class? And, as J. B. Lightfoot pointed out 100 years ago, youngsters are far more logical than their elders. How can Christianity possibly be *the* truth if Christian books tell stories which are *not* true? Those are to blame who first sowed the seeds of doubt — forgetting that while faith may grow like mustard, doubts grow like mushrooms.

It is instructive to compare what Professor Hunter wrote in *1945* with what Dr. J. A. T. Robinson wrote in *1977*:

Hunter:

'Scarcely a reputable scholar in this country is prepared to affirm that the Fourth Gospel was written by John the Apostle.' ('Introducing the New Testament').

Robinson:

'I have come to find apostolic authorship . . . the hypothesis which presents the least (sic) difficulties.' ('Can we Trust the New Testament?').

Obviously, not all scholars share Dr. Robinson's opinion; but the fact that after 30 years *some* have come full circle back to the traditional view demonstrates, I think, how wrong it is to brainwash children into believing that these matters have been settled once and for all by the 'scientific' expertise' of our century.

Finally, another quotation from J. B. Lightfoot. Though written with reference to *Supernatural Religion*, every word could as well be applied today to the Cambridge Bible Commentary on *John*:

'Even if it be granted that the opinion of Irenaeus as an isolated individual is not worth much, yet the widespread and traditional belief which underlies his whole language and thoughts is a consideration of the highest importance: and Irenaeus is only one among many witnesses. *The author's treatment of the external evidences to the Fourth Gospel is wholly vitiated by his ignoring the combined force of such facts* as these. A man might with just as much reason assert that a sturdy oak sapling must have sprung up overnight, because circumstances had prevented him from witnessing its continuous growth.' (our italics).

The Fourth Gospel — Authenticity

A. *Objections based on style*

I. *The similarity of the Gospel to the Epistle (I John):*

'In I John there are 67 echoes of the Gospel; John's distinctive style is apparent in both the Gospel and the Epistle; *therefore* clearly the Gospel is an ideal reconstruction, not factual history.'

Answer

A disciple is not above his teacher, nor a servant above his master.

1. Which is more likely:

a. that John's style of thinking and writing produced a novel and fictitious Jesus?

or

b. that Jesus's style of teaching deeply and permanently influenced John's?

2. Let us compare other Epistles with other Gospels:

i. James with Matthew. He has 30 echoes of the Gospel (17 of the Sermon on the Mount).
Which is more likely: that James wrote the Sermon and put it (fraudulently) into Jesus' mouth? *or* that Jesus preached the Sermon and lodged it in James's heart?

ii. I Peter with Luke's Gospel. Peter has 6 references to sheep and shepherding. The word 'flock' (poimnion) is used only by him and Luke (12:32) and Paul (Acts 20:28, 29).
Which is more likely: that Peter invented the Parable of the Lost Sheep, and the teaching in Luke 12, *or* that Jesus actually spoke these words?

3. The obvious *ANSWERS:*

i. James was deeply impressed with Christ's ethical teaching, so he developed and applied it pastorally in *his* Epistle.

ii. Peter was deeply impressed with Christ's teaching on sheep and shepherds, so he developed and applied this pastorally in his Epistle.

iii. *Similarly John* was deeply impressed with Christ's doctrinal teaching (e.g. on Light, Life, Truth etc.), so he developed and applied *these* themes pastorally in *his* Epistle.

4. As one who stood nearer to the Lord than any of the apostles, and possibly the youngest, John probably absorbed his Master's *style* of doctrinal teaching more than any of them. This is confirmed by three facts:

i. The passages Matthew 11:25—27 = Luke 10:21, 22 though not in John are typically 'Johannine'.

So the Johannine style really means Jesus' style of speaking about Himself.

ii. In spite of the 67 echoes of the Gospel in I John, there is not a single O.T. quotation nor an allegory. The manner is still the manner of Jesus, but the matter is the matter of John (and much less *interesting*).

iii.   Words peculiar to the Gospel and Epistle are found in an historical context in the Gospel but generalised in the Epistle:

e.g.   John 8:44 = 1 John 3:15 (murderer)
         John 13:33 = 1 John 2:1 (teknia, children)

Conclusion

It was the style and vocabulary of the Lord Jesus Christ that made John write as he did; it was *not* the style and vocabulary of John that made Jesus speak as He does.

II. *Objection based on the difficulty of distinguishing the author's comments from the speaker's words,* e.g. in John 3:16—21 and 30—36.

The argument runs thus:

1. Not all the words that Jesus 'said' are actually His, e.g. in these verses John tacks on his own theology (a) to the words of Christ (b) to the words of the Baptist.

2. If John tacked on his own theology to one discourse, he may well have tacked it on to others, e.g. in chapter 5, what about vv. 20—23 and 25—29?

3. We can therefore never be sure whether the words are Jesus' words or John's.

4. Similarly the other Evangelists probably added their own interpretations e.g. to the Parable of the Sower.

5. Therefore in all four Gospels we can never be sure which are Christ's words and which are the Evangelist's.

6. All the Evangelists adapted and altered Christ's words (no doubt under the guidance of the Holy Spirit) to suit the needs of 1st century Christians.

7. We have the same Spirit, so we are equally at liberty to adapt and alter the words of Christ to suit the needs of 20th century Christians. 'We must have the courage to say, it is written . . . but I say unto you . . .' ('Soundings' by Cambridge Theologians)!!

Answer to (a) *objection based on John 3:30–36.*
There are solid grounds for affirming that the Baptist *did* speak these verses:

1. He refers to Christ by his usual phrase, Ho erchomenos = the coming One. (cp. Matthew 11:3 and 3:11).

2. The tenses are all present, indicating that the words were spoken during the Lord's lifetime.

3. The words 'no one receives His testimony' would be meaningless after churches had been founded in most cities of the Roman Empire.

4. The word 'wrath' was evidently characteristic of the Baptist's preaching (Matthew 3:7 and Luke 3:7); only once used by Christ, and never by John the apostle in his letters.

It is therefore very probable that the Baptist used it here again.

Answer to (b) *objection based on John 3:16–21)*
1. In all the Gospels Jesus very frequently speaks of Himself in the *third* person: Matthew 8:20; 25:31; Mark 10:45; Luke 19:10; John 5:19; 6:27; 17:3; etc.

2. When John wishes to explain some words of Jesus, he does so in a perfectly straightforward manner, e.g.
   '. . . but He meant the temple of His body.' (2:21)
   '. . . this He spoke referring to the Spirit . . .' (7:39)

'. . . He said this to signify how He was going to die . . .' 12:33)

3. John's comments are clearly differentiated from Jesus' words in 12:36(b)—44.

4. In 21:23 John deliberately refutes the apostles' interpretation of a saying of Jesus and solemnly repeats His actual words.

We may therefore assume that throughout the Gospel John is equally careful to preserve the actual words of Jesus, *not* an interpretation of them.

5. Every discourse is given a historical, geographical and social setting (i.e. when, where, and to whom spoken), even when these seem to add little to the total effect (e.g. 10:6, 19—22, 14:31).

This is a clear token of truth.

Conclusion

There is no reason to doubt that John 3:16—21 contain the actual words of Christ spoken to Nicodemus.

III. *Objection*
'The discourses are reported in precis form, therefore they are more John's words than Christ's.'

Answer
1. We allow that John does omit some parts of some dialogues, e.g. 11:40; 12:34. But the question is not whether what is recorded is the *whole* truth, but whether what is recorded is *nothing but the truth.*

2. The discourses do not read like precis because of the frequent repetitions, e.g. Barrett thinks that chapter 15 is a 'doubtlet' of chapter 14.

Final answer to objections
a. About 123 times in John it is written that 'Jesus said' words which are not reported by the Synoptics.

b. The words 'truth', 'true' and 'truly' occur in John's writings (including the Apocalypse) nearly as often (88 times) as in all other books of the New Testament.

c. *Therefore* if Jesus did not speak these words, the apostle of Truth must be accounted the greatest of liars.

B. *Objections based upon John's 'faulty chronology'*

I. *Cleansing of the Temple:*
   cp. John 2:13—22 with Mark 11:15—18. Are they the same? (see chapter 13 'Doublets')

Answer:
   They are not the same. There were two cleansings of the Temple, as is shown by
   a. The remarkable differences in this account from those in Matthew, Mark and Luke:

   1. Different method — Christ used a whip (who would have invented it?).
   2. Christ spoke different words.
   3. The Jews gave different answers (Matthew 21:16).

   b. The remarkable correspondence of this story with other parts of Matthew, Mark and Luke:

   1. 'Destroy this temple' (2:19) is echoed in Mark 14:57—59 and Matthew 27:40. Matthew, Mark and Luke do not record the first cleansing because they omit *all* the Judaean ministry until Passion Week.

   2. Compare John 2:20 with Luke 3:1:

Tiberius began to reign with Augustus	12 A.D.
Luke 3:1 — fifteenth year	+15
first year of Christ's ministry	27 A.D.
Josephus says the Temple was begun (18th year of Herod the Great)	19 B.C.
(John 2:20) Total	46 years

   therefore either John was a brilliant forger or the story is true. It fits exactly.

II *The day of the Crucifixion — Puzzle A*
1. Matthew, Mark and Luke clearly state that Jesus ate the Passover Supper with his disciples (Matthew 26:17; Mark 14:12; Luke 22:7).

2. John appears to state that the meal was before the Passover (14:1, 29).

Solution

1. The Law clearly distinguishes between the passover supper and the passover feast (Leviticus 23:5, 6; Numbers 28:16, 17).

2. Therefore the passover supper did take place before the Feast of the Passover, exactly as John says.

Puzzle B

John 18:28. Does this mean the Passover lamb?

Solution

1. Ceremonial defilement lapsed at sundown (Leviticus 22:7).

2. The passover lamb was eaten after sundown (Matthew 26:20).

3. Therefore 18:28 does *not* refer to the passover supper and lamb. To what then does it refer?

4. The word 'passover' included all animal sacrifices killed during the week of the feast (Deuteronomy 16:3). Some of these were eaten by *day,* obviously.

So what the Jews wanted to avoid was defilement which would prevent them enjoying their *lunch* on a feast day!

Puzzle C

John 19:14, 31, 42. Does *'Paraskeue'* mean the day before the Passover?

Solution. Look up references in Matthew, Mark and Luke.

1. In Matthew 27:62 it is translated Friday in the N.E.B. Mark 15:42 — 'preparation day', that is, the day before the Sabbath. Luke 23:54: 'it was Friday'.

2. Deduction from these verses: the word *Paraskeue* (= preparation) has lost its verbal force. Nowhere in the N.T. is it used with an objective genitive, i.e. preparation *for* something.

3. In modern Greek the word means Friday.

4. Therefore in John 19 too it must mean not 'the eve of Passover' (NEB) but Passover Friday.

Conclusion

1. There is no disagreement whatever between Matthew, Mark Luke and John on the day of the crucifixion.

2. The idea that John re-wrote the history to make out that Jesus died at the same time as the paschal lamb is *pure fantasy*.

III. *The time of the Crucifixion*

Puzzle: Mark says it was at 9.0 a.m. (15:25, NEB). John says Pilate pronounced sentence at noon (19:14, NEB).

Solution

1. Mark uses Jewish time (16:1). A new day begins in the evening, so in Mark 15:25 the N.E.B. is right.

2. John uses Roman time (20:19). After dark on Sunday was still 'the first day of the week', so in John 19:14 the N.E.B. is wrong.

It should read: 'It was Passover Friday, about 6.0 a.m.'

C. *Further confirmation of the authenticity of the Gospel*

John's Characterisation i.e. portrayal of minor characters.

1. John's Gospel is only 5/6 as long as Matthew's but he has nearly twice as many words spoken by individuals (human, not angels or devils) other than Christ (John 1235: Matthew 628).

2. There are 19 of these speakers:

A. *Those who speak in Matthew, Mark and Luke*	B. *Those who do not speak in Matthew, Mark and Luke*
John the Baptist	Nicodemus
John the Apostle	Samaritan woman
Martha and Mary	Man born blind and parents
Peter	Man at Bethesda
Pilate	Philip and Andrew
Judas Iscariot	Thomas
	Caiaphas
	Nathaniel
	Judas not Iscariot
	Mary Magdalene

3. List B obviously cannot be checked against Matthew, Mark and Luke but they are all thoroughly self-consistent characters.

4. The recorded deeds and words of the people in List A agree very well with their characters as sketched by Matthew, Mark and Luke — especially Martha and Mary, Peter, Pilate.

5. Therefore *either* John was a brilliant literary artist, anticipating Shakespeare by 15 centuries, or he simply told the truth.

Conclusion

If John was able to remember[1] exactly the words of minor characters, *how much more* would he have accurately remembered the 'ipsissima verba' of Christ.

A final question

'That John (the apostle) is really the author of the Gospel, and that no other planned and completed it than he who at all times is named as its author, cannot be doubted or denied, however often in our times critics have been pleased to doubt and deny it on grounds which are wholly foreign to the subject: on the contrary, every argument from every quarter to which we can look, every trace and record, combine together to render any serious doubt upon the question absolutely impossible.'

Heinrich von Ewald (1803–75), 'one of the foremost German orientalist and theologians of the 19th century' (EB) as quoted by B. F. Westcott, *Introduction to the Study of the Gospels.*

---

1. In saying this we by no means exclude mechanical aids to memory. 'In my own time', says Seneca, 'there have been inventions of this sort . . . *short-hand*, which has been carried to such a perfection that a writer can keep pace with the most rapid speaker.' (Seneca was a Roman philosopher contemporary with the Apostles.)

Church Fathers

Papias, Bishop of Hierapolis (Asia Minor, 135 A.D.)

'And the elder said this also: Mark, having become the interpreter of Peter, wrote down accurately everything that he remembered, without however recording in order what was either said or done by Christ. For neither did he hear the Lord, nor did he follow Him; but afterwards, as I said, (followed) Peter, who adapted his instructions to the needs (of his hearers) but had no design of giving a connected account of the Lord's oracles ('kuriaka logia'). So then Mark made no mistake while he thus wrote down some things as he remembered them; for he made it his one care not to omit anything that he heard, or to set down any false statement therein.'

Justin Martyr (100–165 A.D.)

Born in Samaria of pagan parents, was converted at Ephesus after years of seeking truth through philosophy. Thenceforth he went from place to place preaching Christianity — especially to educated pagans. At Rome he lectured for several years and wrote his 'Apology' and 'Dialogue', which include about 120 allusions to the Gospel-history and 16 times mention the 'Memoirs of the Apostles'. Some examples:

1. '. . . the Apostles in the Memoirs made by them, which are called Gospels, handed down that it was thus enjoined on them . . .' (explaining the celebration of the Lord's Supper).

2. '. . . Memoirs which I say were composed by the apostles and by those who followed them (i.e. as companions).'

3. '. . . the Memoirs of the Apostles or the writings of the prophets are read, as long as the time permits.' (when describing a Christian worship-service).

Bishop Westcott comments:

'. . . the identification of his Memoirs with our Gospels seems to be as reasonable as it is natural.' (CNT p. 117)

Tatian (110–172 A.D.)

Was born in Mesopotamia of Syrian parentage and educated in Greek learning. At Rome he became a Christian through Justin Martyr's teaching, but afterwards adopted a Gnostic heresy and preached it in Syria and Asia Minor. His most famous book was a *Harmony of the Four Gospels* or *Diatessaron* (published at Edessa, now Urfa in Turkey), which became very popular but was later proscribed by .Bishops as being tainted with heresy, and disappeared from view. Critical scholars of the 19th century struggled hard to maintain that it was *not* a harmony of *our* four Gospels, but when an actual MS was discovered in the 1880's, all their ingenious theories had to be abandoned and the church tradition was shown to be unquestionably true. The *Diatessaron* begins with the first five verses of John's Gospel.

Irenaeus (120–200 A.D.)

Was born in Asia Minor; in his youth a keen disciple of Polycarp, who had been appointed Bishop of Smyrna by John the Apostle. Later he emigrated to Lyons where he became a presbyter and then Bishop, after the terrible persecution of 177 A.D., during which he happened to be in Rome. A successful evangelist, an earnest peacemaker between Christian factions, and a voluminous writer, his most famous work was *Against all Heresies*. Few Christians of his day had better opportunities for learning all that had been 'handed down' concerning the Gospels, both in the West and in the East. His testimony is as follows:

'Now Matthew published among the Hebrews a written Gospel also in their own tongue, while Peter and Paul were preaching in Rome and founding the church. But after their death Mark also, the disciple and interpreter of Peter, himself handed down to us in writing the things which were preached by Peter; and Luke also, who was a follower of Paul, put down in a book the gospel which was preached by him. Then John, the disciple of the Lord, who had even rested on His breast, himself also gave forth the Gospel while he was living at Ephesus in Asia.'

Clement of Alexandria (155—220 A.D.)

Was born of non-Christian parents, probably at Athens. 'No heathen contemporary shows such a power of memory or so wide an acquaintance with the classical culture of Greece' (J. B. Lightfoot). Like the merchant seeking goodly pearls, he travelled widely and learned from Christian teachers in Greece, Asia Minor, Palestine and Italy, finally settling in Alexandria as a pupil of Pantaenus, founder of the theological seminary. When Pantaenus left for India, Clement succeeded him and taught from 189 to 202. His later years were spent in Caesarea and Jerusalem. A prolific author, he wrote in defence of Christianity against heathenism and of orthodoxy against heresies. His opinion regarding the Gospels, based upon years of research and fellowship with churches throughout the Empire, was as follows:

'. . . those Gospels were first written which include the genealogies, but the Gospel according to Mark came into being in this manner: When Peter had publicly preached the word at Rome, and by the Spirit had proclaimed the Gospel, those present, who were many, exhorted Mark, as one who had followed him for a long time and remembered what had been spoken, to make a record of what was said; and he did this, and distributed the Gospel among those that asked him. Last of all John, conscious that the outward facts had been set forth in the Gospels, was urged on by his disciples; and, divinely moved by the Spirit, com- ·posed a spiritual Gospel.'

Tertullian (155—222 A.D.)

'. . . after Augustine the greatest of the ancient church writers of the West' was born in Carthage, son of a Roman centurion, and converted to Christianity in mature manhood at Rome. Trained as a lawyer, he turned his talent to good account by propagating in vehement rhetorical Latin the truths which he had studied in Greek (i.e. the Bible, the writings of Justin, Tatian, Irenaeus, Clement, and many others). So great was his reputation for genius and learning that later church writers always speak of him with high respect.

Concerning the Gospels he has this to say:

'We lay down as a principle first that the evangelic instrument has apostles for its authors, on whom this charge of publishing the Gospel was imposed by the Lord himself; that if (it includes the writings of) apostolic men also (i.e. Mark and Luke), still they were not alone, but (wrote) with (the help of) apostles and after (the teaching of) apostles. In fine, John and Matthew out of the number of the apostles implant faith in us, Luke and Mark out of the number of their followers refresh it.'

Origen (185–254 A.D.)

'The foremost writer of his age', (J.B.L.), was at once the most learned, the most widely-travelled and the most influential Christian between St. Paul and St. Augustine. Born of Christian parents at Alexandria, he lost his father at 17 in the persecution of 202 A.D. and in 203 became Clement's successor as head of the theological seminary. He is said to have employed six stenographers and to have written 6000 books — commentaries, exposition of Scripture, and refutation of heresy. His travels included visits to Rome, Arabia, Palestine and Antioch; also Greece, Cappadocia, and Nicomedia (near Istanbul). His lectures and methodical teaching were famous for fifty years. No one had better opportunities for gathering information from Christian documents and congregations in scores of churches over a very wide area. During the Decian persecution he survived imprisonment and torture and died at Tyre — indefatigably zealous to the last.

His *account of the Gospels* is as follows:

'. . . having learnt by tradition concerning the four Gospels which alone are unquestionable in the Church of God under heaven, that first was written that according to Matthew, who was once a tax-collector but afterwards an apostle of Jesus Christ, who published it for those who from Judaism came to believe, composed as it was in the Hebrew language.

Secondly, that according to Mark, who wrote it in accordance with Peter's instructions, whom also Peter acknowledged as his son in the catholic epistle, speaking in these terms: "She that is in Babylon, elect together with you; and so does Mark my son."

And thirdly, that according to Luke, who wrote for those who from the Gentiles (came to believe), the Gospel that was praised by Paul. After them all, that according to John . . . who leaned back on Jesus' breast.'

Eusebius (260–340 A.D.)

Bishop of Caesarea (where St. Paul was imprisoned), scholar and writer, his books are 'the chief primary source for the history of the Church up to 324 A.D.'; also for most of these mini-biographies (p. 135 ff) and the quotations appended.

He took particular care to record the judgment of the Church on all the books of the New Testament, dividing them into two classes — the 'acknowledged' and the 'disputed'. Among the 'acknowledged', he writes, 'in the first place should be put the holy *tetrad* of the Gospels'. (This 'tetrad' was the special word used by the Pythagorean school of philosophers to denote the number 4 as *'the root and source of all things'* (Liddell & Scott, *Greek Lexicon*). It suggests that Eusebius was well aware of the supreme importance of the four Gospels as foundational to the Christian faith).

In the previous chapter he writes: 'Matthew had first preached to Hebrews, and when he was on the point of going to others he transmitted in writing in his native language the Gospel according to himself. After Mark and Luke had published their Gospels . . . John was asked to relate in his own Gospel the period passed over in silence by the former evangelists.'

Eusebius' History runs to 500 pages, which should be required reading for all ordinands. Link by link he forges a

chain of solid historical evidence connecting the faith of the
Church in Acts with the faith of the Church in his own time.
Next to a thorough study of the Gospels in Greek, a good
strong dose of Eusebius is the best possible antidote to the
heady hypotheses and dogmatic doubts of modern critical
scholars.

Bibliography

The abbreviations shown thus: (AWA) or (CWTNT) after author or title are those used within the footnotes to the text.

A. Modern critical scholars

Professor D. E. Nineham (DN), *Saint Mark,* Pelican NT Commentaries.

A. W. Argyle (AWA), *Matthew,* Cambridge Bible Commentary (CBC).

Professor A. M. Hunter (AH), *John,* Cambridge Bible Commentary (CBC).

Dr. J. A. T. Robinson (JR), *Can we Trust the New Testament?,* (CWTNT), Mowbrays.

A. E. Harvey (AH), *Companion to the Gospels,* Oxford/Cambridge University Press (OUP/CUP).

B. Conservative scholars

Eusebius' *Church History,* Loeb edition.

A. Carr, *St. Matthew,* Cambridge Bible for Schools.

G. F. Maclear, *St. Mark,* Cambridge Bible for Schools.

A. Plummer, *St. John,* Cambridge Bible for Schools.

B. F. Westcott (BFW), *Introduction to the Study of the Gospels.*

B. F. Westcott (BFW), *History of the NT Canon.*

M. R. James, translator, *Apocryphal New Testament,* Oxford University Press.

J. B. Lightfoot (JBL), *Essays on the work entitled 'Supernatural Religion'.*

Jamieson, Fausset and Brown (JFB), *Commentary on the whole Bible.*

R. C. Trench (RCT), *Notes on the Parables.*

R. C. Trench (RCT), *Notes on the Miracles.*

J. C. Ryle, *Expository Thoughts on the Gospels,* 1860/70,
James Clarke, Cambridge, still in print and still one of the
best.

C. Others

Encyclopaedia Britannica (EB).
G. Orwell, *Animal Farm* (AF).

D. Books supporting the literal interpretation of Genesis 1–11
   (See Chapter 20)

Whitcomb and Morris, *The Genesis Flood,* Evangelical Press.
A. J. Monty White, *What about Origins?,* Dunestone Printers.
D. C. C. Watson, *Myths and Miracles,* H. E. Walter.
D. C. C. Watson, *The Great Brain Robbery,* H. E. Walter.
Biblical Creation, published three times a year by the Biblical
   Creation Society, c/o Dr. C. H. Darnbrough, 21 Alnwickhill
   Park, Edinburgh.